YOUR MARRIAGE COMPANION

SECRETS TO MAKING YOUR RELATIONSHIP WORK

ISHOLA AND DORIS FAMILUSI

Your Marriage Companion, Secrets To Making Your Relationship Work

Copyright © 2017 Ishola and Doris Familusi

ISBN 978-0-9928168-2-7

Divine Call Publishers

All rights reserved. No part of this book may be reproduced without prior written consent of the publishers.

"All Scripture quotations, unless otherwise indicated, are taken from the Holy Bible: King James Version(KJV)"

DEDICATION

This book is dedicated, first of all, to Almighty God who has inspired, enabled and strengthened us to write it. Not only is He the Author of this institution called marriage; He has designed it to work as we follow His pattern.

We also dedicate this to millions of married couples out there, who, instead of giving up, are doing all it takes to make their marriages work. Your marriages are destined for greatness. Keep working at them.

ACKNOWLEDGEMENT

We want to thank everyone who has been a part of making this book a reality.

Marriage4Life community, your continuous support ensures that we remain relevant in reaching out to marriages.

We are grateful for our family and siblings who have stood by us. To our children Temi, Tobi and Asher who have been extremely patient with us as we committed time to this book.

We are grateful to all those who have worked with us in transcribing, editing and overall production of the project.

Finally, a big thank you to our couple friends who have submitted their Honest Advice to Married Couples. Their various perspectives add a rich flavour to the completion of this book.

FOREWORD

It's a joy and an honour to write a foreword for the first printed book from Marriage4Life- YOUR MARRIAGE COMPANION. My husband and I have been privileged to be in close relationship with this amazing couple, Ishola and Doris (founders of Marriage4Life); since 2008. Married for 17 years (and still counting!), they've both been a great example of God's plan for partnership in marriage- labouring side by side in building their home, Rockchurch and the Kingdom of God at large.

This isn't just a book, but it's also a working and very workable manual for a highly successful marriage! It contains 16 'juicy' chapters- covering every area you could think of, and even goes beyond your imagination. It's very unusual to find a book that addresses all important areas of your marriage; the invaluable topics like- Ingredients For a Successful Marriage, Couples' Danger Zone, Marriage Misconceptions, 7 Things Your Marriage Cannot Live Without, Anger Management & Resolution, Communication and Sex, etc; make this book a one stop book!

My husband and I will be 30 years in marriage next year (2018), by God's grace, and have been jointly involved in Ministry for those years; and from our rich experiences in marriage and Ministry, this is a book I would HIGHLY recommend to anyone who is serious about enjoying a happy and successful marriage.

I would love to personally commend the hard work, sacrifices, commitment, openness and honesty that have been put into this timeless manual. Thanks for pouring your heart out into this book; and for not holding back from being such a terrific blessing! May God pour back to your lives, your marriage and Ministry; and may you finish strong, in Jesus' name. Rev. Kola and I are so proud of you.

Don't just read this book, but also make sure you recommend and share it with others! God bless you.

Rev. Funke Ewuosho.

Fountain of Wisdom Ministries.

FIRST WORDS

Hello, everyone! Welcome to the very first printed publication from Marriage4Life. What God is doing through this ministry is simply amazing.

Ishola and I recently celebrated seventeen years of marriage, and we thank God for how far He has brought us. Reaching this milestone helped us realise we have a lot to share about maintaining a lasting and successful marriage. This book aims to give you some tips on improving your marriage. We know we have benefited from its contents and we hope you will too. Please bear in mind that this information is based on Christian and Biblical perspectives.

All Scripture references have been taken from the King James Version (KJV) of the Bible unless otherwise stated.

OK! Batten down the hatches, let's go!

Table of Contents

ACKNOWLEDGEMENT v

FOREWORD vii

FIRST WORDS ix

CHAPTER ONE: WHY I GOT MARRIED
(AND I'M STAYING MARRIED!) 1

CHAPTER TWO: INGREDIENTS FOR A SUCCESSFUL
MARRIAGE 9

CHAPTER THREE: SPEAK LIFE INTO YOUR MARRIAGE 19

CHAPTER FOUR: COUPLES DANGER ZONE – HOW DID
WE GET HERE? 29

CHAPTER FIVE: MARRIAGE MISCONCEPTIONS 39

CHAPTER SIX: WMRW VS. WWRW 51

CHAPTER SEVEN: 7 THINGS YOUR MARRIAGE CANNOT
LIVE WITHOUT 63

CHAPTER EIGHT: ALL I WANT FOR VALENTINE'S IS… 71

CHAPTER NINE: CHILDBIRTH AND CHANGES TO A
WOMAN'S BODY (CONFIDENCE CRISES) 79

CHAPTER TEN: ANGER MANAGEMENT & RESOLUTION 85

CHAPTER ELEVEN: 5 REASONS MARRIED COUPLES
SHOULD HAVE SEX REGULARLY 99

CHAPTER TWELVE: COMMUNICATION AND SEX 107

CHAPTER THIRTEEN: YOUR MONEY, MY MONEY – OUR MONEY 117

CHAPTER FOURTEEN: SIX FINANCIAL MISTAKES COUPLES MAKE 133

CHAPTER FIFTEEN: HOW TO PRAY FOR YOUR SPOUSE 137

CHAPTER SIXTEEN: HONEST ADVICE FROM MARRIED COUPLES 147

STRENGTH IN COMPROMISE 179

ABOUT MARRIAGE4LIFE MINISTRY 183

THE CONCLUSION OF THE MATTER 187

CHAPTER ONE

Why I got married (and I'm staying married!)

What is God's definition of marriage and how does He want us to view it?

Society recognises marriage as the highest level of commitment, but it's more than that. It's one of the most beautiful, yet most challenging things that could happen in a person's life. It is the highest level of commitment mandated by God. The Bible calls marriage *honourable*, and states that: "what God has joined together, let no man separate". This is how highly God esteems your marriage. Marriage is God's idea, God's design, and therefore He backs it if it's left in His able hands.

In case you thought it was nothing to write home about, God values your marriage. You might not be walking an easy road, but you have something to be proud of. If you're thinking as you read this book:

You have no clue. My marriage looks great on the outside, but it is an absolute mess, welcome to the club. God values your marriage, whether it is currently sweet or dry and in need of watering. The good news is, God is committed to whatever He values. He has good plans to ensure that whatever He holds to heart prospers. Jeremiah 29:11 says: ***"For I know the thoughts that I think toward you, saith the LORD, thoughts of peace, and not of evil, to give you an expected end."***

Marriage gives men and women the opportunity to accomplish their desires for genuine companionship, affection, security and procreation. No wonder most people, whether they admit it or not, desire to be married. Marriage allows you to 'do' life with someone else. Sharing the burdens of life makes them lighter and sharing the joys of life makes them sweeter! For the Christian, not only is marriage a gift from God, it allows us to build a relationship based on love and faithfulness. ***Two are better than one; because they have a good reward for their labour.*** (Ecclesiastes 4:9)

I got married because I met a man who, despite all my imperfections, loved me for who I am; which made me decide to spend the rest of my life with him. I wasn't perfect. I loved myself most of the time, but on quite a few days, I had so many insecurities and questioned so many things that I didn't really know who I was. Thankfully, he could demonstrate to me and others that he loved me. I sometimes didn't understand why, but he showed me time and time again that I needed to view myself, not through my inadequacies, but from his loving perspective.

God sent His only Son to die for us IN SPITE OF our sin and disobedience. When you pray for a spouse, He will always lead you to someone you need and teach you how to love them the way He loves us.

...But God commendeth his love toward us, in that, while we were yet sinners, Christ died for us. (Romans 5:8)

After all the hurt and pain of my past, God gave me someone who loved me unconditionally. I had to marry him just for that.

I also got married because I wanted to model God's pattern. I had seen different sides of marital relationships, and I wanted to reflect God's style of marriage. I grew up in a polygamous home in Nigeria. My father had several wives, and my perspective of marriage was dysfunctional. After I had become a Christian, I realised this wasn't what marriage was meant to be and made up my mind that God could use me to showcase His ideal for marriage. Your experience may be similar to mine, or you may look at your parents' marriage and lament that their relationship is nothing like what the Bible says it should be.

Marriage is not simple, easy, or a walk in the park. It is complex and requires a lot of hard work and enormous commitment. One really needs to think about these things before entering into marriage. Believe me when I say that conflicts occur and challenges come along. My husband and I have had our share of disagreements over the past seventeen years, but with God's help and our willingness to sacrifice for each other and our relationship, we've gotten through them, and we are still learning, growing and developing. It is a continuous process that, if handled wisely and biblically, gets better and better as you grow together. In marriage, you need to understand that there will be various times where you will have to disagree to agree or agree to disagree. You should get to a place where you both decide on what conflict resolution looks like for you as a couple, as this will take your marriage forward. It's no longer about 'what makes ME happy', but 'what makes US happy'.

Marriage can be great! You may presently feel as if that's not true, but God's word assures us that it is possible. There are numerous couples enjoying their marriages out there and having a lot of fun. They may make it look easy, but actually, they've decided that, despite what they go through, or the disagreements they get into, they will trust God and prayerfully work towards resolving their issues.

The third reason I married Ishola was that we were so in love, it just made sense to us to get married. You know how some things in life have a natural progression? One thing will naturally flow into the other like a spring just flows into the river and a river to the sea. Well, our relationship was like that. We loved each other so much, had eyes for no one else, and couldn't see us spending our lives with anyone else. We both felt God had placed us in each other's lives, so we decided it was right to get married. Our decision to marry was not without opposition, though.

Have you ever made a major decision, only for people around you to keep second-guessing your choice? That happened to me. I got married at twenty-five, which was a problem for my family who believed that I should have been obtaining a Master's and possibly a Doctorate degree. Marriage could wait. Other well-meaning friends had the same idea, so I had a lot of people asking me, "Are you certain you want to do this?" "Are you sure you guys are ready for this step?" "Are you sure this person is right for you?" People might question your decisions: whether it is 'should you get married', 'should you stay married', or something to do with your state at that moment. Most people have good intentions, but deep down, *you know* the answer. For every situation, you will have deep convictions about what you need to do. The most important thing is to be sure it fits with what God has assured you is His will, and plan for your life before taking that decision.

Why I got married (and I'm staying married!)

If you do decide to get married, be warned: every day is not the same. At first, it's all lovey-dovey, *I am for you, you're for me; we are going to have so much fun*! Everything is wonderful, and every day is bliss. However, there will be occasions when things don't go your way, and you'll often need to compromise. There will be times when you question your decision to get married. Recognise, however, that being happy is <u>A CHOICE</u>. If you want a marriage that displays God's glory you can have it. All you need to do is ask Him to step in now and make what He wants out of your marriage. Be an example for those in your circle of influence, amongst family and friends, in church or at work. Let them witness God's ideal marriage through you and want this for themselves. We want them to see that it is possible to be married, stay married, and enjoy their marriage.

My husband and I are still learning things about each other, but we know we love each other and wouldn't want to be with anyone else. I've been blessed with a spouse who is willing to communicate with me, talk things through, love me despite my flaws, pray over me and treat me like his queen.

So, I'm staying married because I'm destined to enjoy the fruits of every labour over my marriage. Be encouraged to stay married – it may be hard work, but it's also thoroughly enjoyable.

Action Points:

1. List your reasons for getting married and staying married.

2. In what practical ways could each of these reasons strengthen and deepen intimacy in your marriage?

CHAPTER TWO

Ingredients for a successful marriage

In the previous chapter, I touched on why I married and am staying married. I explained that it wasn't easy and takes a great deal of hard work. There are certain ingredients which, if present in your relationship, will help you succeed. I want to share some of them with you in this chapter. These ingredients have definitely been the keys to our marital success, in addition to the main pillar — God!

Ingredient No. 1 - **LOVE**

The world's definition of love does not sustain a marriage. Unfortunately, marriages based on this kind of love fail because people happily step into it, but hastily jump out when things don't go their way. Sometimes physical looks, situations or finances change. Whatever the issue, the shallow love some have based their relationship on doesn't last and they eventually quit. Love that is based on physical elements or feelings alone cannot sustain commitment in a marriage. Feelings come and go! You may feel up this minute and down the next. Temperamental love is not sufficient to build a lasting marriage.

The kind of love that will sustain a marriage is *AGAPE,* God's unconditional love that, despite ourselves and regardless of what happens, will not stop loving us. Agape causes us to say, "I love you", and goes on when the wrinkles appear, after two, three, or more children, after the physical attraction has waned. Agape is love that acts, endures and honours. It says, "I love you because Christ commands me to". Agape is enduring love. It is not here today and gone tomorrow. Even during the dry seasons when you're not happy (yes, every marriage has dry seasons), Agape will sustain your marriage. It is this love that helps you see your spouse the way Christ does; love that embraces, regardless of the circumstances. It propels you to love even when it feels like you shouldn't, or you think they don't deserve it. This is AGAPE.

Ingredient No. 2 - **HONOUR**

To honour is to **VALUE the other person**. It means to respect, admire and to think highly of a person. It also means to fulfil an obligation or to keep an agreement. We ought to honour our spouse. What you value, you will honour! When you value what you have, its merit increases and you celebrate it! So, when it comes to your spouse, nothing and no one ought to look better. You shouldn't think about that person you could have married five, ten or thirty years ago. Your spouse becomes the most valuable gift God has given to you. Over the past seventeen years, my husband and I decided we would see each other in this way, and it has sustained us. MARRIAGE BLOSSOMS WHEN WE MARRY THE ONES WE LOVE AND EVEN MORE SO WHEN WE LOVE THE ONES WE MARRY.

Some people say that the grass is greener on the other side. This is usually false. The grass is probably greener because its owner is giving it the care and attention it needs; watering, fertilising, weeding, and making sure it is cut neatly. On the other hand, it could be that you don't notice when animals make a mess on it or when brown patches that need work appear. You probably aren't close enough to see the areas that need extra care. All you can see from your own lawn is the lovely greenery in your neighbour's garden. Some say the grass you see looking so green may just be AstroTurf.

What you see looking so alluring elsewhere doesn't make what you have any less beautiful. When you treasure what you have, nothing can stop you from protecting it. You can never rubbish anything that you cherish. Pay attention to what you have and value it. Honour your spouse; love and respect them. When you appreciate what you have, God expands it and makes it bigger, however, if you don't value what you have, sooner or later you will lose it.

Ingredient No. 3 - **COMMUNICATION**

This is one ingredient couples shouldn't play around with. Talk and then listen! If you don't talk, you will explode. If you don't listen, you'll miss important lessons. It is crucial for spouses to talk to each other. You both need to express how you feel. Some of us

Ingredients for a successful marriage

do all the talking in our marriage without allowing the other person to get a word in edgewise.

Some spouses don't feel free to express themselves in marriage. They have insecurities and fear that if they express their feelings, they would be punished for their opinions or what they say. If your wife says, "I'm lonely", to you, Husband, please note she is only telling you how she feels. Accept it and don't start giving reasons why she shouldn't be lonely. See what you can do about it. Wife, if your husband says, "I want to be looked after a bit more", instead of giving him reasons why he shouldn't feel that way, be open and try doing something about it! Have you ever considered asking your spouse: "Hey Hon, how can I make your day better today?" My husband and I do this every so often. He tells me what I can do to help him be the man he wants to be, and I tell him likewise what he can do for me. We talk! Make sure you're talking.

But please find the right time and healthy ways to do this. Earlier on in our marriage, my choice of words in communicating with Ishola especially when I felt upset about a particular issue made me come across to him as harsh. I sounded like I was attacking him, so he became defensive and less receptive to whatever I had to say. I would, in turn, become even more upset and the situation would literally blow out of proportion. Now, I mind my word choices; so I would say something like: "I feel like we haven't been as close lately", instead of "you have been distant with me lately". When talking try using 'I' and 'we', instead of 'you'.

Do not underestimate the power of communication in marriage. This book encourages you to share openly and honestly with each other. Don't bear grudges. Talk, and in so doing, release each other from the offence.

Ingredient No. 4 - **CELEBRATE YOUR DIFFERENCES**.

Yes, I said celebrate them! My husband and I are complete opposites. As a couple, you may find this to be true for you. You probably came from different parts of the world, and have families, economic backgrounds and values that are dissimilar. Instead of allowing those differences to make you tear each other down, find ways of celebrating them and building each other up.

These three key areas may vary. Our NATURE - who we are, our NURTURE – how we were raised, and our CULTURE – the environment and way of life in which we were brought up. I will give you an example: I come from a lively household, but Ishola's background is a lot quieter, so communicating is done differently where he comes from. This meant that when we got together, I had to unlearn some things which I considered normal. I had to recognise when I could speak bluntly and when I needed to be diplomatic. You're never too old to learn new things or to unlearn habits you've practised for so long. Ishola also began to speak up and not hold back when necessary. Not everything you bring into your marriage will work, and so it is important to be open to embracing differences and change.

Ingredient No. 5 - **COVER YOUR SPOUSE**.

When I was younger and living in Nigeria, an elderly lady gave me some advice which I still cherish today.

She said to me, "Don't let people fool around with you and your husband. If he is quiet, they will try to take advantage of him. Don't stand for it. Speak up!" I have found this to be very true and stood by it throughout our married lives. We deal with things in very different ways, and while I celebrate his calm manner and disposition, there is no gain in allowing others to take it for granted. I am not advocating being loud, boisterous, or generally harsh. What I am saying is, be assertive and, when it is called for, accept no nonsense. Love, protect your spouse and don't let anyone take advantage of them. Your differences can work for you in more ways than you realise.

Ingredient No. 6 - **VERBALLY APPRECIATE EACH OTHER ALL THE TIME**.

We can't say this one enough! Your spouse would love to hear from you. A phone call, text or other verbal communication is always welcome. They can't read your mind, so make sure you let them know they've been great with whatever it is that you appreciate so much. Even if there is nothing specific, send a "just because" message.

Ingredients for a successful marriage

The seventh and final ingredient is to **BUILD AND MAINTAIN A FRIENDSHIP**.

This is a very, very important one to ensure you have. It will help your marriage survive, even in times when things seem dry between you and your spouse. Friendship and marriage go hand in hand. One cannot work without the other. You shouldn't just be lovers; you need to be friends. In a friendship, you're more vulnerable, and guys love that because you've made them your "safe haven". They love that they are someone with whom you can laugh and share jokes.

So, there you have it, seven key ingredients to a successful marriage. Bear in mind, though, that these aren't exhaustive and there are others that haven't been mentioned in this book. The most important one, however, is the **Agape Love of God**. Once your marriage is built on this, and you take these little pointers onboard, you can stay happily married for a long, long time.

Action Points:

1. Which of the seven ingredients set out in this chapter already happen in your marriage?

2. Can you think of simple ways to improve on them? How will you implement these?

3. Which ingredient(s) is/are not yet happening in your marriage? Create and begin to implement a list of clear-cut ways to turn this around.

CHAPTER THREE

Speak Life into your Marriage

We decide how and what we speak into our marriage. Whether they are words of life and positivity or death and negativity – the choice is ours. This chapter will be looking at words from a Christian perspective and how to speak life into your marriage.

Every good marriage has a lot of good words spoken in and over it, while bad marriages have the opposite. Surprisingly, these are not the only options. Dead marriages have no words at all. Whatever we speak comes back to us.

Let's look at a few passages of Scripture and study what they teach us about words and speaking.

The first passage is Proverbs 18: 20-22:

A man's stomach shall be satisfied from the fruit of his mouth, from the produce of his lips he shall be filled. Death and life are in the power of the tongue, and those who love it will eat its fruit. He that findeth a wife finds a good thing and obtaineth favor from the Lord.

Verses 20 and 21 clearly state that our tongues, and by extension, the words we speak, have the power to give life or command death to situations. Now, how does the writer go from speaking about death and life in the power of the tongue to discussing marriage – a seemingly unrelated topic (v.22)? Understand that the words we speak are very, very important. The Bible says whatsoever a man sows, that shall he reap (Gal 6:7). Like a farmer planting seeds and aiming for a harvest, we reap what we sow into our marriages. Whatever we say is what we obtain. Moving in any direction from wherever we are now is very dependent on the words that we speak. We, therefore, need to be intentional about what we say.

Good words

These are sweet, loving, fantastic words of encouragement. Good words cause growth and development. They encourage trust and a sense of security and help us build faith, not fear. Throughout the Bible, there are many examples of good words that couples can speak to and over each other. They are there for every situation – you simply have to look, and you will find them in plain sight.

Everybody is moved by words, and every response in life can often be traced back to verbal or written words.

The Bible says the words we speak are spirit and life. Therefore, words are alive and active, powerful in their execution. In the long run, every spoken word achieves its purpose, so be conscious of this fact and ensure that the words you speak are only ever positive and good.

No wonder the vehicle through which God has given us access to excel in life is His WORD (the Bible) which is also called THE GOOD NEWS!

Bad words

These are words that hold no merit. They pull down, discourage, emasculate and denigrate. Bad words hold no life, joy or peace. They do not encourage friendship, foster growth or deepen love. Bad words cause us to develop fears and hold secrets because they breed dissatisfaction and cause distrust. God does not like it when Christian couples use these types of words with each other. It's part of the reason why we had the reminder about the power that lies in your tongue right before the Scripture: "whosoever finds a wife finds a good thing". Bad words will not only destroy a marriage but destroy destinies. Let's be cautious and avoid negative words in and around our marriages.

No words

For those who don't communicate and have no words, these are the dead marriages. They have no life because they have no words.

> *A man's stomach shall be satisfied from the fruit of his mouth, from the produce of his lips he shall be filled. (Prov. 18:20)*

The above verse is not only referring to physical fruit (produce) or being physically full. There is also a spiritual and marital aspect. If you consider your words as the fruit of your mouth—a fruit being the outcome of the tree—this means that it is possible to enrich your marriage with the positive outcomes of your mouth! Clearly, this verse is showing that what we use our tongues for, bearing in mind that the Scripture also says, "Death and life are in the power of the tongue", will either make or mar our marriages.

The words we speak are so important. They can build us up or tear us down. Have a close look at the Word (Bible) and see how God wants us to use our tongues to build up our marriages, children and homes. Conversely, the devil wants us to use that same tongue as a tool to destroy what God is building in our lives. The path we follow is our choice. Our marriages will not rise above the level of our verbal confessions or the words spoken over it. Our tongue affects our home, so be careful not to give the devil a foothold.

There are numerous reasons why people speak bad words. Some of us are from backgrounds where that is all we know. We, therefore, pick that up and take it into our marriage. My background is a bit like that, and as I grew up, I did not realise I was internalising this negative way of speaking. Despite my being a quiet person who didn't speak much as a youngster, I still learned to speak the wrong things, and as such, the first and second years of our marriage were nearly disastrous. We spoke such harsh words to each other. I especially (and more often) said things I didn't realise I knew how to say. Of course, I later discovered that it was what I had assimilated growing up.

Our past plays a great part in how we are conditioned to direct our future. Some of us may have been through terrible parental or romantic relationships that did not end well. As a result, you may have made a vow never to open up certain parts of yourself to anyone again. However, now that you're married, certain feelings and words keep coming up whenever there is a difference of opinion between you and your spouse, and in using negative words to safeguard yourself, you hurt your spouse and replicate your past. Such insecurities, and I mean ALL OF THEM, need to be handed over to God Who can help us align our tongues, so we are making the best use of them in our marriages.

Galatians 6:7 - *Be not deceived, God is not mocked: for whatsoever a man soweth, that shall he also reap.*

Words are like seeds and only what we plant will grow. You cannot plant negative words expecting to reap positive reactions. Similarly, it is impossible to plant positive words and reap negative reactions. Verse 8 in the NKJV goes on to say:

> *"...for he who sows to the flesh, will of the flesh reap corruption; but he who sows to the Spirit will of the Spirit reap everlasting life".*

Sometimes you might be tempted to speak the wrong words to your spouse due to something that you are going through, or you being unhappy with them at that point. However, there is no excuse for speaking harshly because our response to what comes our way is our decision.

We should not respond harshly when challenges

arise - that should not be our first reaction. We need to discipline ourselves to speak life, even when we face contrary circumstances. Our first instinct is usually, "I want to get back at you because you have hurt me", but replying with anger and revenge doesn't help. Others tend to respond with passive aggression, so the hostility is not overt, but in your heart, you are actually saying, "I'm going to ignore you and not do whatever you want me to". Then there's the silent treatment. This is a clear situation of no words, which leads to dead marriages.

I was told once of a situation where a husband and wife had argued. At the end of the argument, she went off to do the housework and began singing a worship song. He heard her and started to join in. However, she got upset and thought, *"how dare you join in? This is my worship song, not yours! Don't sing it!"* This is not the right attitude. She may not have voiced what she was thinking, but the passive aggression was present. Harbouring it closes the door to reconciliation and forgiveness.

The beauty of speaking good words is that the results will always be positive. Everyone responds well to kind words. Everyone loves compliments, we all love praise and like to be told when we are doing well or that we look nice and things of this nature. We prefer mellow or affirmative responses as opposed to dark, angry, derogatory statements. When you speak good words to your spouse, you can receive a phenomenal response. Make up your mind to speak good and fruitful words that you want to germinate in your marriage. Get to know each other's love language and speak it every day. Do this and watch where God will take you.

Words have a way of exposing what is in your heart. Sometimes we say something and then think, "Oh, but I didn't really mean that," but the Bible says the mouth speaks from the abundance of the heart (Matt 12:34). Let positive words be planted and germinate in your mind, heart and mouth.

Additional Scriptures to study:

Matthew 12:33: *Either make the tree good, and his fruit good; or else make the tree corrupt, and his fruit corrupt: for the tree is known by his fruit.*

If you find yourself constantly speaking damaging words to your spouse, check your heart for bitterness or unforgiveness. Something in you needs to be dealt with, and once it is done, God will use this situation to heal your marriage.

Matthew 12: 36-37:

> *But I say unto you, that every idle word that men shall speak, they shall give account thereof in the day of judgment. For by thy words thou shalt be justified, and by thy words thou shalt be condemned.*

Be careful. The words you sow will definitely germinate and be reaped.

Action Points:

1. How can you ensure that 'good' words become a steady pattern in your marriage?

2. List some ways to eradicate 'bad' words in your home.

3. How can you protect your relationship from reaching a place of 'no words'?

CHAPTER FOUR

Couples Danger Zone – how did we get here?

A relationship is like a building. There is a design showing how it should look, from which you carve out a solid foundation, place footings, lay the foundation, then build the walls, place the windows, doors, etc. If you've done it right, you'll have a structure to last a lifetime.

Now, did you know that a building doesn't suddenly collapse? What happens is, cracks initially appear because there is a fault with the foundation that was laid. These cracks keep opening and become gaps, which then widen, and it gets worse and worse until the building eventually collapses.

There are times within our marriages when we put ourselves in places that we're not even aware of. It happens ever so slowly, and one day we discover that we have drifted apart or that things aren't going the way they should. At this stage, you begin to cheat on your spouse. Cheating doesn't only refer to sexual immorality, but to those periods when you don't give your spouse the time or kindness they require, but you give it to someone else. We don't need to wait until the marital cracks become gaps, or indeed until the building crumbles before we do something about it. In this chapter, we'll look at some of the danger zones and show what can be done to secure the foundation, repair the walls, and keep your marriage on track.

1. ***Give less attention to technology.*** These days, couples give more and more attention to mobile phones, television, the Internet, X-Box, etc. It is important to make time for your spouse and make that an investment. The time you set aside for your spouse, should remain for your spouse. We are not necessarily referring to dinner times when you are serving or being served. We mean other times when you put your phone away, shut down social media, and close the emails. Give them your full attention and TALK! (I am very guilty of this

one, and am constantly asking God to change me and help me do better!)

Watch a movie TOGETHER. Play a game TOGETHER. We've all had that moment when we're on a date, and a call comes in or a text or something of the sort, and we're off on the phone again. Just say NO to distractions and interruptions when you've set time aside for your spouse. Strengthen your bond and relationship.

2. ***Never give your leftovers to your spouse.*** How do we do this? If we take the example of someone in a customer facing position at work or perhaps someone from church. You smile and greet others warmly, but when it comes to your own spouse, you cannot muster even a little smile. All you give them is attitude and surliness. In the same manner that you can smile and be lovely to complete strangers, smile at and be real with your spouse. Communicate effectively with them to let them know how you feel. Don't scowl

and shut them out. Spouses shouldn't have to deal with our poor attitudes. Try your best to be loving towards them despite how you're feeling.

3. ***Try not to spend more time with your friends than you do with your spouse.*** Time is the currency of any relationship, so it's important to spend more time with your spouse. If you hang out more with your work colleagues, girlfriends or mates than with your spouse, your marriage will suffer. And in the same way, if you make time to do with your spouse what you do with your friends, your marriage will be sweeter and more enjoyable.

This is not to say you can't have friends or value the time you spend with them. Understand, however, that on getting married, you chose this one friend over all others and they deserve to be treated in an honoured manner. Set and keep boundaries. Feel free to build meaningful friendships around your work, church, and anywhere else where you serve or work. This especially applies to ladies. Ladies generally need to have other persons we can trust and talk to but don't wind up overwhelming your husbands with everything that goes through your minds, hearts and emotions. It will be too much for him! Men need meaningful and healthy friendships as well, but set boundaries and stick to them. Don't be the person who neglects your spouse to favour friends. In fact, if your friends don't understand that you need to prioritise your spouse, you should carefully consider if you want to keep their friendship. They should know how to respect your marital relationship — that's a big deal!

4. *No secrets!* It's already been said, but let me reiterate briefly. There should be no secrets between you. There is no reason why your spouse should not have your passwords, for example. If you need to keep your passwords a secret, ask yourself why and deal with it. You should be completely open with your spouse. Remember, secrets are a hindrance to intimacy. All couples need to operate in

truth and openness. Let's face it, we all have baggage, and we drag this heavy weight along, right into our marriages. The funny thing is, we then try to hide this big old bag! Even funnier, sometimes, we're successful at doing so.

There is no one without vulnerability or insecurities. However, when you come into the marriage covenant, you need to be willing to open that heavy suitcase and let your vulnerability and insecurities be seen. Every pocket with every secret, hurt, pain, and area of distrust needs to be turned out so you both can be real with each other. This openness is fantastic for your relationship overall, and for intimacy within the marriage.

5. *Never flirt with anyone other than your spouse.* It's rather easily done, isn't it? Both at work and when we go out, we sometimes get into conversations that can become flirtatious. At times these conversations can lead to something bigger—like adultery. I'm not

talking about overt conversations (although you should not be having those either). What I mean are the subtle conversations where things are 'suggested but not quite said'. What happens is, ever so slowly, you find yourself drifting apart from your spouse. The cracks appear, and the gaps start to form. Then the big collapse suddenly happens! Notice, it didn't start as a big thing, it started subtly.

Suggestive conversations, from over-complimenting to unnecessary texting or over-friendly banter, can be toxic and damaging to fidelity in marriage. You should feel uncomfortable with things of this nature and discuss them with your spouse if they occur, as they can really get out of hand. Stay away from them.

6. ***Do NOT compare your relationship with other people's.*** It is very discouraging to constantly compare your husband or wife to someone else. We need to avoid this as much as possible. There is no perfect marriage;

people are fickle, and we all have faults. The secret to avoiding this danger zone is to come together, get to know each other and build yourselves up. It helps if you research some of the things that are required for marriage before going into it, and once married, arm yourself with the necessary information to deal with problems as they arise.

My best advice for staying in marital safe zones is to pray continually. Ask God to strengthen your marriage and help both of you improve your relationship with each other. Let Him be the one to examine you, and make any changes or turn you inside out. See the good in your spouse and focus on it. This is not to say you won't discuss any negative aspects, after all, positive communication on negative actions is important. Focus on the positives, and find a way to speak words of life regarding any negative aspects of your marriage.

My final word on danger zones is this; prayer will keep you away from danger. I'll say it again; prayer will keep you away from danger. Remember to pray for your spouse. Pray for yourself. You will also need to change and, yes, it can be challenging, but with God's help, you can pray in the right way to make your marriage better.

Action Point:

1. Considering your individuality, how can both of you make sure you never fall prey to any of these danger zones?

CHAPTER FIVE

Marriage Misconceptions

We have been in ministry for some time now. We've had the opportunity to connect with wonderful and resourceful persons, and from time to time in this book, we will be sharing some of the advice shared by them.

In our time of counselling, teaching, preaching and sharing, we have encountered numerous misconceptions about marriage while interacting with people. The most common one we have heard comes from single people:

> ***I believe marriage will bring an end to my loneliness, or the lack of happiness, joy or fulfilment in my life.***

This is a huge misconception. So, if you are single and reading this book thinking marriage is going to resolve all your personal insecurities, let us be honest with you – it won't. But read on. Also, if you are married and thinking you made the wrong choice, read on. This book aims to give you the tools you need to overcome these hurdles and be successful.

As we have discussed before, marriage often happens between people from different backgrounds who may have been raised differently. Coming together means both parties bring their baggage which includes past hurts, pain, unhappiness and insecurities into the marriage. Unfortunately, many find this out quite soon *after* getting married and struggle to get through the challenges they then face.

The only way to combat and overcome these obstacles is **<u>introspection</u>**. You need to look inside yourself and make the necessary changes. Marriage is hard work. You must discover yourselves and work out your marriage. It is not simple, but it can be very exciting and very fulfilling if you proceed with the right attitude.

One of the first things we advise is that you change your mindset and adopt the understanding that your love for God can make you truly happy. You need to first be fulfilled in God, and from that platform, other areas in your life will be fulfilled as well. No man or woman can satisfy you the way God can. Our fulfilment in life is God's job. This is why no man or woman can fill this space. God never gives us a gift that will take us away from Him. Of course, your spouse should make you happy, but seek God's presence and guard it, for in His presence is the fullness of joy. Marriage is a partnership. People sometimes separate, citing incompatibility or irreconcilable differences. This happens when the butterflies of *getting* married have all gone away, and the hard work of *staying* married begins.

The truth is, you are not happy every day! No one on this earth can make you happy every single day throughout a lifelong commitment. The emotions you feel going into a situation may lead you to believe that you have reached a stalemate. But wait, pay attention!

The first step to developing your relationship is to be FRIENDS with your spouse, so that when the butterflies stop fluttering, you can rekindle that and love can bloom. If you base your relationship on fluttering butterflies, you are building your entire relationship on passing emotions. When you reach the point of giving it all up, please don't think you are no longer compatible or that you are no longer feeling the love. Work on your friendship – this is what marriage is made of. Finding love is one thing, sustaining it requires hard work and commitment from both parties in the relationship.

Here is another misconception we've found.

If I marry the right person, the emotions will remain throughout the marriage.

We wish this were so, but it's not actually the case. The emotions will be there at the beginning, but when you start to live together as man and wife and get to know each other; you will see all the faults and flaws which were always present but veiled before the wedding. Sometimes it is the case that you were so much in love and high on emotion that you were blind to those faults. Or you didn't want to see them.

Now is the time to work on getting the right knowledge. Knowledge is important because, if you don't know much about the psychological differences between men and women before marriage, your spouse will do so many things which you will not understand. If you already know men are wired one way and women the other, you can apply that knowledge to various situations. This helps during the times when you start to feel, 'perhaps I've not married the right person'. Knowledge will help you understand that this is a lie and that you have indeed married the right person. Learn and develop your spouse's love language. The strong emotions may not be there, but if you learn to show love in a way that is unique and meaningful to them, you can continue being friends and work on your relationship. You will eventually see an even more beautiful dynamic blossom within your marriage.

Love is an emotion which you must make a conscious decision to share with someone. Too many marriages crash because people say they are no longer in love. There may be times when you feel happy and joyful, and others when you are sad and down, but that does not change your personality. Love is a decision. When you marry someone, you choose to love them for life, regardless of whether your feelings are there or not. It is possible that over time some of your intense feelings will initially fade, but to remain married, you need to continuously acknowledge that you have committed to stay with that person for life. To make your marriage last, you do not need to be perfect, just be committed.

The things we do together also determine how we can become comfortable and trusting with ourselves as friends. You need to be able to relax with and make your spouse laugh because that is where the air of comfort with each other comes. Love can spring again from this. Like a fire, if it dwindles, all love needs is one hot ember to re-spark the flames. Love, therefore, is beyond the feelings or emotions. We emphasise this: **it is a conscious decision to love my spouse for the rest of my life.**

Psychologically it often seems more difficult to forgive those who are closest to us. It is said that this is because we love them more. Let me give you an awesome truth:

Marriage stands when you can forgive and let go readily.

You forgive in advance. If you cannot do this as a matter of course, it is a great thing to learn. Understand that this person is going to upset you, but know that you will forgive them. There are certain things that you do and assume are acceptable, for which, actually, you need to be forgiven. Always try to put yourself in their shoes. Learn to be forgiving and do it in advance.

Several things can be done to keep the flame alive in your marriage. Couples need to deliberately have their romance on top spec. Things like having frequent date nights. If we use our relationships with our churches as an example, those of us who are committed to church attend frequently and not just on Sundays. We go on Sunday, then midweek, perhaps volunteer for some other church activity during the week, attend life groups, etc. By spending time with others in church, you are building up a relationship with them. How much more your own marriage and spouse?

Doing activities with your partner has also got to be intentional. Whether it's once a week or however frequently you decide, that time should be set aside. You do not need to break the bank to do it; you can choose simple pleasures like chatting at the table or watching a movie on TV. Put the technology away, and the children to bed, and have some "us" time.

Misconception number three:

If so much effort is required to make the marriage work, I'm not joined to my soulmate.

Nothing could be further from the truth. Soulmates are not born, they are made. Great marriages don't fall from the sky.

Consider the butterfly. It starts life as an egg, hatches into a caterpillar, then metamorphoses into a pupa and finally struggles its way out as a butterfly. The struggle it goes through to become a pupa, gaining weight and spinning all that chrysalis around it isn't easy, but it is necessary. Also at the stage of coming out of the pupa, the butterfly must fight so its wings can be strengthened. If that fight doesn't happen, the butterfly will never fly. Similarly, your marriage should go through the same process so as to 'fly'.

Thinking you won't have to work hard at your marriage, is also like saying if your business is meant to succeed, you won't have to work very hard to make it happen. For anything being handled by people with emotions and feelings to succeed, you realise you have to selflessly put something into it to get something out of it. In the same way that you work hard on your business and don't just fold your arms expecting miracles to happen, immense effort is required for a successful marriage. It's got to be 100%! The Bible says its with the same measure you sow that you will reap.

In the book of Ephesians, it also says husbands should love their wives like Christ loved the church and gave himself for it. So, husbands should learn how to lay their lives down for their wives, and in this way, wives would learn to submit to their husbands. As you grow and learn more of each other, God helps knit you together and there your soulmate is made.

The saying goes: 'love is all you need', however in marriage, it's only one of the things you need. There are a few pillars required to hold your marriage together such as:

Love – is pivotal to every relationship.

Deep Respect – most women believe the number one need for men in relationships is sex, but respect is what men want most. Deep respect will help you see your spouse as who God wants them to be. Even if they do something that seems silly, respect their choice and ask 'why' later.

Patience – we need to take the time to know and find out what makes each other tick.

Honour – is one of the things God requires from everyone, whether in or out of marriage. This pillar is very important to maintain a servant heart in marriage.

Endurance – the ability to face tough situations and stick them out to a better result.

Tolerance – The Bible says love does not fly off the handle. If there is tolerance in relationships, there is nothing that cannot be overcome.

Marriage Misconceptions

Focus – Being single-minded and having eyes only for your spouse.

Being non-judgmental – the ability to listen objectively to your spouse's opinion or perspective without trying to force yours on them.

Trust – Our marriage cannot rise above the level of our trust for each other. You must intentionally fight to keep trust and seek restoration when it is broken.

Communication – women tend to want to do this more, while men do it to get the short answer.

Bearing the above in mind, we advocate learning more about the opposite sex by studying and acquiring knowledge so that you can relate to your spouse more effectively. God made us the way we are, and it wasn't a mistake. For example, if the wife is having a bad day, the husband may see that she's moody, but have no clue why, even if he's in the house with her and she's 'dropped hints' about what's happening. While she's thinking 'he should know what's going on and help out!' she gets angrier by the minute, and he is still clueless. Women, we need to SAY!

Communicating sensitively is also essential. Yes, you can point out things that are not desired, but do so in a respectful manner. Most men will respond well to correction if it is done in a respectful manner. Words, once spoken, cannot be retracted.

So, before you jump into your relationship, talk. Talk about your expectations, fears and ambitions. DON'T ASSUME or this will lead to areas of uncertainty.

The best way to overcome misconceptions is to do things God's way. Your faith will be stronger and you will experience greater success.

Action Points:

1. Write out some ways couples can overcome each misconception listed in this chapter.

2. How have these misconceptions affected your own mindset concerning marriage?

CHAPTER SIX

WMRW vs. WWRW

No one goes into marriage to fail, everyone wants to succeed. However, we know it's not as simple as that, and as women, we want to get it right. So, before I explain what *women* really want, I've asked my lovely husband Ishola, to share what *men* really want with us from his perspective. Enjoy!

What men really want (WMRW)

The first key thing is that men like to be **honoured and respected.** We don't like to be bullied or nagged because of our personality types. When our wives confront us unwisely, it comes across as nagging or bullying, or that they always want to have their own way. Men are crazy for honour! When a man is honoured and respected, he will always perform better and want to be there.

Now, it sounds strange, but this honour and respect needs to stretch to the point where you <u>allow him to fail</u>. That's right. Allow him to make *his* mistakes and learn from them, even if you knew this would be the result! God has given you intuition, which means that you can 'see things' men cannot. In a bid to try to help your husband succeed, you get involved – but the way you do so can come across as nagging! Even if your husband cannot see what you see, allow him to explore. For us, if something we do doesn't work, it's not a failure - it's an **ADVENTURE**. We are adventurous and want to try, so let us try – even if we fail. Support and help us learn, and you'll soon see that one of the things we learn is to <u>listen to you</u>!

The way you present things to your husband is also important. Most times it's not WHAT you say but HOW it is said. If you honour him enough, you will know how to effectively frame your words and confront him with issues. Even if he still thinks otherwise, let GOD be the Enforcer. Allow God to enforce the right thinking on him. If you have clarity on a matter, but he still doesn't, pray about it! In most cases, God will visit us (men) and let us know that you are right.

Every woman has a dream of where she wants her husband to be. Honour him as though he is there already and he will become what you perceive him to be.

Hebrews 11:1 AMPC: Now faith is the assurance (the confirmation, the title deed) of the things [we] hope for, being the proof of things [we] do not see and the conviction of their reality [faith perceiving as real fact what is not revealed to the senses].

Men love praise and encouragement! Wives, learn to cover our faults in prayer and concentrate on our strengths. Focus on the good, as the good in our lives outweighs the faults. Note, however, that we don't like to be compared with other men — that can kill our zeal in marriage.

What drives most wives to nag is FEAR! Fear that your husband won't become what you want him to be, and thinking that things won't work for you as a family if he doesn't become the idea you have in your head. We don't doubt that your intentions are good, but we ask that you pursue them with FAITH in God, knowing that He can make us (your husband) what you and God want him to be.

The second thing is **sex**. Most men are more sexual than their wives. Maybe in about 20% of relationships, wives are more sexual, but men mostly have higher desire levels. Male stimulation is physical and visual. Husbands want their wives to be sexually alluring all the time. We love to see our wives with nothing on, so while this may be out of your comfort zone, learn to let your husband appreciate you. Look good for him. Keep his heart racing! Don't think you've been together for so long you don't need to bother. Make the effort! Go shopping, get something that will visually stimulate him and keep his juices flowing. When you keep his juices flowing, you will always have him with you.

A little note to men:

Never compare your wife with others who did not bear the pain of having children for you. See *your* wife, love, appreciate and respect her.

Men, another tip for you is: rather than sex being just 'another event', do a bit of preparation for your wife to be turned on. You know, we're straightforward and just want to get on with sex in our 'ready to act' way, but women need a bit more. They need romance and the works, so the event can happen *and* be enjoyable.

How do you prepare? Communicate with your wife through the day. You can text, email or call her. Men aren't great at communication, but we need to learn how. We are programmed to act, to DO, not listen and talk. It's not easy to find the balance, but it is possible. Do some verbal training beforehand. For example, you could call and interact with her during the day, which engages and gets her attention. Look at it like this, if you were an athlete participating in an event, you don't just show up and perform. There's all the training weeks or months beforehand, strategies, the right dietary requirements, and then you appear for the game, warm up and play. So, up your marital game!

Women, if your husband is visually stimulated, he will be excited just to get home to be with you. It's extremely valuable to keep the marriage spiced up.

The third thing men want is **a companion they can open their hearts to**. Men by nature can be very guarded about their feelings and emotions, so they feel VERY bruised if they are betrayed. If a man cannot trust you, he cannot pour his heart out to you. The best way for your husband to trust you is for you to be his friend. That way he sees you as his haven.

Be your husband's friend, not a mother. You may be the mother of his children, but I implore you to resist the temptation of going into maternal mode on him, as it will cause him to resent you. Fulfil your role as his friend and helpmeet. Your husband will only ever have one mother, and you are not her.

Step out of your world and into his for a bit. What does he enjoy doing? What keeps him happy and motivated? Do some of those things with him. When you enjoy his world with him, he will be as open as can be with you. Men usually let it all out when they are having a good time, so learn to have a good time with your husband. Encourage him with what he likes because he wants to enjoy sharing it with you and having fun with you. Be that person, and he will be convinced that whatever he shares with you is safe in your hands.

Finally, men love **the support they get at home**. After going to work for the day, they want to come back to a home and not a house. Women need to learn how to make it warm and homely for him. Check the way it's decorated. Also, what sort of environment are you allowing to permeate? He doesn't want to come home to an unkempt wife; neither does he want to return to an untidy home, he wants to come to a clean, calm and peaceful place.

Prayerfully do your best to adhere to the advice given and watch your husband become a very satisfied man.

What women really want (WWRW)

It's now my turn to share from the wifely perspective, so keep reading, Husbands!

In marriage, the husband and wife should try to meet each other's needs, but how can men serve their wives better? They recognise that when they have a peaceful home and wife, they have a peaceful life. So what things should they do to make and keep their wives happy?

Firstly, **a woman wants to feel secure in her husband's love**. She needs to feel and be assured that she's the only one for you. The way you care for her should show your sacrificial love, as you give and lay down your all for her. This does not in any way mean you now have no life or that you forget about your family and friends. No! It only means she's priority. God first, your wife next, all others come after. Women need to be able to sense that they are number one, and of course the only one for you. We don't want to feel like we are competing with anyone. Ephesians 5 says men are to lay down their lives for their wives. That's the level of security we look for. Your wife is to be the love of your life, and the only one who is deeply connected with you. Show the world that you have chosen her and no other.

The second thing is: we need **to know that our husbands are sensitive to our needs**. That they are moved by whatever moves us, be it emotional, physical, financial or spiritual. The more sensitive a husband is to the needs of his wife, the more sexually attracted she is to him! Don't ask me why or how! It's how we're wired.

The third thing is **the need for communication**. Guys, you need to learn how to communicate with us. If you want our relationship to work, then learn to talk with me. When a husband is open and talks with his wife, he is saying he trusts her. It's this special connection that a woman loves. Women love to download information, so when she asks you "how was your day?" she wants actual details, not a monosyllabic "Alright" or "OK". She needs you to share with her. A woman will pick up undertones as you talk; she's sensitive to how you say what you say. We want our husbands to connect with us on a level deeper than sex, beyond anything physical. Go beyond the bedroom and learn to talk. Don't hide things from us. Share. We feel valued and loved when you share fully with us.

Fourth is **non-sexual affection**. Now here's the kicker! For us, sex is not the goal. Touch our shoulders or hold us around the waist, stroke or hold our hands, hug and give us pecks on the forehead or cheek without sex being the goal. We don't always want it to be about physical sexual activity, we're more interested in the trusting intimacy that non-sexual affection creates. Most times, however, if you give this non-sexual attention, you will get what you actually want! No woman wants to feel like every time her husband touches her, it winds up in sex. Non-sexual affection makes us feel <u>valued</u> and not just as a sex machine; she may want to be this sex machine, but she wants to be more!

Finally, we want **our husbands to be the leader**. When it comes to family decisions, romance, sex, even with spiritual things, be the one who starts. We don't want to initiate everything; you begin something. Don't wait until we're talking and talking (I know, you call it nagging!). Understand how to get things going. We like it when you pray over us or even speak over us. Not just during family prayer time, but, for example, in the morning, take our hand and speak God's favour over us. We love that! Don't wait for us to initiate conversations, start them. Let's take an evening stroll on a summer's day, be creative in how you show us you care. Romantic gestures don't have to be expensive.

Understand that your making an effort to make us happy is enough for us. When you communicate what you're doing to make us happier, this will rock our world!

Action Points:

1. How eye-opening has this chapter been to your understanding what men and women **really** want in a marriage?

2. Write down practical ways that have helped or will help improve your marriage.

CHAPTER SEVEN

7 things your marriage cannot live without

God – He must come first.

Having God in your marriage makes such a difference. If husband and wife are both doing their best to please God, they will wind up pleasing each other. You will meet at the apex of the triangle, after starting at the opposite angles at the bottom. Faith allows you to pray together and for each other. The Bible says God is love, so the more of God that's in your marriage, the more love will be in your home.

Another part of this is being an active part of a healthy church that stands on, teaches God's word unapologetically, and encourages its members to live by Biblical principles. Prayer is also vital under this heading. Remember that your marriage is an entity that needs covering. We get so engrossed in the other aspects at times that we forget to pray for it. Pray for each other and rain God's blessings into your marriage. We cannot go through the many challenges that we face as a couple without prayer and sometimes intercession. When God is at the centre of your relationship, it is steadfast, cannot be broken or stopped. He builds character in you both to make you the best husband or wife you can be.

Transparency

You both need to be emotionally and physically open with your spouse. A husband should be free to communicate how he feels about his wife or any given subject, without fear of retaliation, judgment or backlash, and vice versa. There should be no secrecy between you; ranging from passwords on your phone or online accounts to everything else. It's about being open, honest and vulnerable to and with each other, which improves intimacy. When you keep secrets from your spouse, they form a barrier that keeps you from responding appropriately when they touch you intimately. As you practice transparency over a long period of time, you will be able to read your spouse's countenance and know whether everything is ok or not.

So, NO SECRETS – Transparency is required.

Kindness

We can reach a point in our marriage where kindness and gentleness fly out of the window. We become very harsh with our spouse both with words and deeds. Do you know what I mean? We get to the stage where we become so comfortable that we take each other's presence for granted and become complacent. At work, for example, you're all smiles with everyone else, being kind and considerate. Then you get home, and you're unkind and moody again! How wrong is that? Or what about if you go to church together, the drive to church is silent, the atmosphere so thick you can cut it with a knife, but you get there, and you're hugging and laughing with everyone except your spouse. If this is the case with you, you need to sort that out as it is crucial. Treat your spouse like you would treat an accepted stranger. We smile and welcome them, show them our good side, and even try to impress them. Remember little things like opening the door for your wife, or serving your husband first. Let kindness and gentleness reign in your marriage.

What sorts of things are we talking about? For example, your spouse is trying to explain something, and you have an idea what they're going to say, hear them out instead of cutting them off with a sharp, dismissive response. Or, husbands, be practical. Help with the dishes, cook sometimes. Wives, how about offering to help wash the car? Never get tired of pleasing each other. Kiss each other. When you're leaving, kiss each other, when you get back, kiss each other.

Sex

Men love this one! Lovemaking is a great spice for a colourful marriage. Without it, your marriage will be very bland. God created and ordained sex for married couples to enjoy, so make the most of it. Science has proven that couples who regularly have sex are healthier, have healthier relationships and are happier in their marriages. A great sex life = a happier couple.

What do you do to have a great sex life? There is always so much going on in our lives: work, kids etc., but you need to be deliberate about getting physical with your spouse. Prepare yourself. Someone suggested having a specific day in the week. If this works for you, then prepare yourself mentally, physically and emotionally for that day. Put on something special, take out the sexy underwear, wear their favourite perfume or cologne, get a little something as a gesture, play some mood music, and think about a special food or snack. You see, sex is not just another activity, particularly for ladies. It's about creating the right atmosphere and properly preparing to enjoy a fantastic time with one another.

Communication

What breathing does for your lungs, communication does for your marriage, in that your lungs would collapse without breathing.

The live wire of marriage is communication. You need to talk about deep as well as trivial things. What's the point of getting married if you won't communicate? This pillar means different things to husband and wife. It's easier for the wife because women want to talk. We want to come in and be a part of your world, and we want you to be detailed about the information that helps us do so. Men, make the extra effort to learn to communicate and open up your world. You may be tired, but one word from her with a different perspective may breathe life into something you were mulling over. Then you'll be refreshed.

Also, don't get tired of saying 'I love you' to each other. Guys, this applies to you more than to women. They need to hear it over, and over and over. Yes, you've said it millions of times, but they need to hear your heart, affirmation and love in words.

Laughter

When last did you laugh with your spouse? A good, hearty laugh over funny things? Even things your children did in the past that were not funny then, but for which you can now look back and thank God with laughter for the grace that kept you through it all. Laugh together at your silliness as well. It breathes positivity and changes the atmosphere. Laugh about the world, your failures, laugh with the kids. The Bible says a joyful heart is like good medicine, but a broken spirit dries up the bones. Marriage should have more comedy than drama.

Friendship and Commitment

Friends are loyal to each other. Great friends make for great relationships and best friends the best relationships. This does not mean you don't have your differences. Naturally, as you are two individuals, this will be the case. However, because you agree on this element of friendship and commitment to each other, it goes way beyond the differences. The relationship can thrive because you are committed to being friends. Husband and wife should be best friends. This requires a quality investment of time. Just as you spend time with your best friend, spend time with your spouse. Be happy in each other's company. Friends have fun together, talk, laugh, trust, and are loyal to each other. Friends don't mind going the extra mile or making sacrifices.

The couples who stay married for a very long time are not the ones who never had arguments or differences; rather they are the ones who value their commitment to and friendship with each other MORE than the reasons to separate. They believe in the sacredness of 'what God has joined together, let no man put asunder'. That keeps the marriage going and makes things get better and better.

There is no perfect marriage, but you can have a great marriage if these 7 things are present in your relationship.

Action Points:

1. Does your relationship currently enjoy the seven items listed above?

2. If not, in what practical ways can each one begin to feature in your marriage?

3. How can you further deepen and protect them?

CHAPTER EIGHT

All I want for Valentine's is...

Every year, this remains a very popular season when couples have an opportunity to celebrate the love between them. It's great that it falls in the early part of the year, as it gives a chance to reflect, rekindle and set goals for the remainder of the year.

Some people look forward to Valentine's Day, so they can show outwardly what they inwardly feel to the person they are married to. We also recognise that some do not like this season. It's not compulsory, so if you don't want to, you don't have to do anything special. I personally believe this is a great time to celebrate for the right reasons.

Valentine's Day is **not** a national day of apology. It's not a time to bribe your way to sex or rewards. Couples ought to do their best to maintain a great relationship all year round and celebrate the victories over your struggles on Valentine's, not habitually behave badly, then use the season as a sort of escape clause or "get out of jail free card". A great Valentine's gift you can give your mate is a change of character.

Believe it or not, the best present you can give your spouse is **YOU**!

If your spouse has your heart, then gifts given and received make sense. Also, did you know that every day can be like Valentine's Day in your marriage? Not with the spending, the gifts and such like. I mean, come on, life happens. We work, have children, hobbies and other responsibilities. However, that Valentine-like atmosphere can be created every single day. The atmosphere of care, love and honour that makes your spouse thrive can be achieved. It is vital to give this an important place in your marriage. Everyone deserves to be cherished.

Romance is the cornerstone of marriage and is critical to its survival. Some people believe that only women are romantic, but that is FALSE. We all need romance and to be romantic. What romance looks

All I want for Valentine's is...

like to women differs to how men may view it. It promotes relational skills in marriage, and gives it life! Some people also believe romance is seasonal. Again, this is FALSE. You control the romance in your relationship and pitch it at the level you want it to be all the time.

There are ways to make your Valentine's affordable and not break the bank. Here are a few suggestions:

1) An indoor picnic

2) Movie night at home

3) A sunset stroll in fine weather

4) Springtime flower spotting

5) Wintertime snow fights, followed by hot cocoa on the sofa

6) Cook a meal or bake something together

7) Take a one-off dance lesson

8) Create a chronological collage of your journey together

The important fact is that you be present with your heart.

Most people cannot stand pretence, and unfortunately, in many relationships, the acting is ramped up because it's Valentine's. No! Just be real! If you know you could do with a personality change, do it and make it real. Honesty is a very desirable trait. As married couples, you can use this season to bring about the marriage you desire. Shape the way you want your marriage to go forward, the things you'd like birthed, and use this season to plant the seeds. Then water them as you go along.

Marriage is emotionally bilingual, which means you need to learn each other's love language. Use this season to get to know your spouse's better. Consider your marriage as a meal. You may like it spicy while your spouse prefers theirs moderate. When cooking, you need to adjust for each other's tastes. No point cooking a meal with so much spice your spouse cannot taste, enjoy or stomach it. You don't want to make them sick, you want to please them. Some things make your spouse happy, so take the time

All I want for Valentine's is...

to learn how to capitalise on them and make them really happy.

If you're still not sure what you could do, look through the suggestions below. These are great for Valentine's and all year through.

10 goals every couple should make room for annually

1. Spend time by yourself (individually). While doing that, write down how you felt last year went and what you want to see in the new year.

2. Spend time together. Look at what you've written down, put them together and make sure you both feel these things should be done for the year. Agree on them and pray over them.

3. This year, resolve to engage 1:1 with your spouse. Put the phone down, turn off the TV and spend time with them.

4. Be intentional about having more sex. Don't allow for sexual famine. Make sure you're both satisfied.

5. Keep a regular date night. There will be times when it's hard to fit in, but make sure you do. Watch a movie at home, take a walk, or go to dinner or for a treat. Whatever you do, set a time frame for it to happen (weekly, monthly, bi-monthly) and stick to it. Make it a normal, regular occurrence.

6. Attend a marriage retreat, seminar, talk show or conference. Some of them are free so find a good one and go together.

7. Keep a joint marriage journal in which you both write. Keep it somewhere accessible but private, like in a drawer in your bedroom. Make a note of concerns, appreciation, notable events, and love letters.

8. Watch the movie "War Room" together.

9. Celebrate each of these goals once you start doing them.

All I want for Valentine's is...

10. Read a marriage book together. It can be a book on love, marriage, or romance; something that will give more knowledge to help make your marriage better.

Couples challenge: Try a 14-day period of random acts of kindness. See who can out-please the other. Every blessing!

Action Point:

1. Write down your thoughts on how the ideas and suggestions in this chapter could deepen intimacy and improve your relationship.

CHAPTER NINE

Childbirth and changes to a woman's body (confidence crises)

I recently read that only one in five women ever get back to their pre-pregnancy weight. The other four struggle to make it back and some never do.

Husbands, true love leads you to see this lady, pursue, court, ask her into your life and marry her. All this probably happens during your youth, when her confidence is overflowing, and her body is very appealing to both you and her. She's proud of her appearance, and you're overjoyed that she's agreed to be your wife.

Now it's some time later. She's pregnant, her body is stretching and changing, and so are her mannerisms. You begin to wonder: *how do I cope with this?* One thing is certain; she needs you now, more than ever. Dealing with these feelings improperly has led to some women taking their lives. Saying or doing the wrong thing has, and is still making some wives subject themselves to all sorts of operations. If you speak incorrectly to them, they feel like you no longer love them and all they want to do is make you love them again.

Sometimes we are aware of something we should be working through with our mate, but their timeframe for resolving it does not match our expectation. We become impatient and allow bad/negative words/attitudes. Remember patience is a virtue, and a successful marriage requires lots of it. Patience is not just about being able to wait; it is being able to wait while keeping the right attitude.

Ladies, for you, the uncertainty is more about how your body or figure impacts on your self-confidence. You wonder, "Does my husband still love me? Am I still attractive enough to keep his attention?"

What changes do our bodies go through?

1. Belly bulge. This happens because of hormonal changes in the body. Extra fat forms around

Childbirth and changes to a woman's body (confidence crises)

> the stomach area that take time to go down. Sometimes it doesn't move.
>
> 2. Stretch marks.
>
> 3. Skin discolouration.
>
> 4. Spider veins or varicose veins.
>
> 5. Changes around the legs and hips – they widen, and you may see cellulose appear.
>
> 6. Breast size may increase or decrease. During breastfeeding the size increases, but afterwards, muscles that have stretched to accommodate the production and transfer of milk will sag, and breasts may no longer be as pert. The more children we have, the more pronounced this is.

Many women become depressed and self- conscious and don't feel comfortable undressing in front of their husbands in the bedroom especially with the lights on. They become very insecure, develop low self-esteem, and may be more prone to asking, "Do you still love me?"

From the man's perspective, this can be confusing. You may be thinking, "This woman has brought joy into our home and lives. Why would she doubt that I love her?" If you bear the feelings she's experiencing in mind, you'll understand why it's important to reaffirm your love and commitment to her. This will help rebuild her confidence. Women will always be more particular about their bodies than men, so it's important that husbands support their efforts.

Some women do all they can to put things back the way they used to be, but stretch marks and the belly bulge are very difficult to get rid of. When we realise there is something in our lives that we want to alter, we must be patient and allow the change to happen. Remember the change may not have anything to do with eating. Husbands, you will know that we ate before marriage and managed to remain thin, but pregnancy brings a lot of changes which cannot be helped. One school of thought states that if you want something badly enough, you'll do all you can to achieve it; however, we all know this is easier said than done.

Childbirth and changes to a woman's body (confidence crises)

How can husbands support their wives in staying on the right track?

1. Affirm her verbally. Let her know you understand what's happened to her, but you still love her. Sometimes, it may help to let her know you love her more now than when you first met.

2. Don't compare her to others. Put yourself in her shoes. She's spent nine months growing and even longer feeding this new life. She's been stretched, kicked, prodded and pulled. Yet she carries on looking after the home and, in some instances, working. Her genetic makeup is not like anyone else's; she is unique, and her body will react uniquely. Don't chastise or tell her she's fat. That's not helpful at all.

3. If she finds a conducive weight loss program, why not join her? She will feel appreciated.

4. Relieve her of some duties. If you've just come in, take the children for a bit and give her a reprieve. She will love you forever.

5. Compliment her and really mean it.

Accepting that childbirth makes a physical difference to women BEFORE the children come along will go a long way towards husbands loving their wives and appreciating their bodies after the babies arrive. You can be more understanding, supportive and positive with what you say to your wife. One fine way to prepare for this is to speak with her mother if she is still around. Pregnancies differ, but in families, certain aspects of the process will be the same.

Take time to carry out your research so you can be well prepared for what lies ahead.

A happy wife will give you a happy life!

Action Points:

1. In what ways have pregnancy and childbirth affected the health of your marriage?

2. What aspects of your marriage have been impacted by this chapter and how have you positively turned these areas around?

CHAPTER TEN

Anger Management & Resolution

What is ANGER?

Anger is a natural emotion we will all experience as long as we're alive and interacting with others. There are legitimate reasons for feeling this emotion, e.g., someone violates your trust, you're misunderstood, someone shows immaturity, or you're faced with unrealistic expectations. How we manage it or respond to such situations makes a world of difference to our continued social progression. A study done in 2009 showed that continued spousal anger over a period of three years contributed to depressive illness in the other spouse. Therefore, this emotion must be handled properly in marriage if both parties will continue to be comfortable and happy as they go forward together. If you are in a marriage where one person is constantly displaying negative behaviour, being quarrelsome, always ready to fight, never complimentary, very hostile and antisocial; this type of behaviour will negatively affect the person who is subjected to it. Conflict or differing opinions usually initiate feelings of anger, so positively dealing with them is the best starting point for managing anger.

How to deal with it

Good marriages deal with irritations positively. They discuss points of discomfort, listen to the other person's explanations and seek reconciliation.

People in bad marriages bottle up their feelings. There is no discussion, just skulking around, long faces, and sharp or sarcastic remarks, until the volcano effect occurs, and one or both parties explode.

People cover up anger in a variety of ways:

1. Denial. They simply say they're not angry, usually in the words, "No, I'm alright." In reality, they're extremely upset.

2. False peace. People pretend that they want peace at any cost, so they give in rather than

face the conflict. Our advice is: face it, or it will eventually lead to someone completely withdrawing.

3. Keeping track of offending events. Some people make and pocket a mental or physical list of all the things that upset them. They never deal with them, however, and one day, they explode.

4. Developing passive/aggressive behaviour. *I'm not going to talk to you too much, just nod and make slight acknowledgements.* There is a display, but no dealing with the conflict.

5. Sarcasm. You find a punch line for everything.

6. Procrastination. Your annoyance makes you put off resolving or doing certain things in your marriage.

The Bible says in Eph. 4:26 (KJV)

"Be ye angry, and sin not: let not the sun go down upon your wrath…"

Common misconceptions about anger.

1. *If you don't look angry on the outside, you don't have a problem with anger.* This isn't true. You can be raging on the inside, but act very calm and calculated about how you will handle the situation.'

2. *If you ignore the hurt and anger, the feelings will go away.* The feelings will remain unless they are properly dealt with. They have nowhere to go unless you open up and let them go.

3. *When you vent your feelings, then the anger will go away.* Venting is such a negative way of dealing with emotions. One can constructively express their feelings. It doesn't need to be a rant.

4. *Playing the bigger person all the time and not expressing your exasperation won't damage you.* This isn't true. There has to be a time when you stand up for yourself and say the right thing in the right way. Don't ignore your anger.

5. *Your relationship will suffer if your express your annoyance.* This one kills a lot of marriages, especially where the husband has the explosive temper. This makes the wife bottle up everything because his explosion may lead to verbal or physical abuse and she becomes terrified.

Un-confronted anger will consume the intimacy within your marriage. Ultimately, this is what the enemy wants: to tear you two apart and keep you apart. Why? Because he wants God's ideal for relationships to fail. Anger will cut the lines of communication between you, keep you away from each other, from prayer and from the Word.

Health Matters

Ultimately, if anger is undealt with, your health will be affected. Scientific studies show that unresolved anger more than doubled the risk of having a heart attack. Eph. 4:26–27 encourages us that, as soon as we start to get angry, sort out and resolve problems then and there. Sometimes, if this is done, you may realise that thing wasn't worth getting that cross about in the first place. Holding on to things about which you later explode in the heat of the moment can lead to your angrily recounting past issues that you'd been bottling up. Things which not only happened long ago but may be completely unrelated to the matter at hand. At other times, an action, statement or something else from your spouse triggers the memory of an unresolved situation from your past. Your spouse may have acted innocently, but the unresolved matter makes you explode.

Did you know that depression starts when your emotions can't function anymore? Depression means there's anger and fear deep down inside. These must be dealt with if we want a smooth relationship in our marriage. How do we do this?

1. Admit you're angry. The first step to healing any emotion is admission. If you don't, it takes away your peace. Some people may feel unnecessarily guilty for being angry. Whether your anger is justified or not – admit it. You may very well be wrong, but at that moment, it doesn't matter. You have an emotion that

needs to be dealt with and not bottled up, so just admit you're angry.

Express your feelings in a positive and constructive way within an atmosphere of openness and honesty. Doing it any other way leads to the other party becoming defensive. This can be made easier when you simply allow each other to be human – after all, human beings experience both positive and negative emotions.

2. Walk away in the heat of the moment. This takes a high level of maturity. Sometimes it's difficult to be level headed or constructive when you're exasperated. The best thing to do is walk away for the moment and revisit the matter when things are more settled, and you've had the chance to think things through. Even when your spouse is yelling: "You're always walking away! Come back and deal with this!" Stop for a moment and assure them that you will deal with the matter when you've calmed down and can be more rational, but keep going.

There are two types of angry persons. First, there are the Intimidators. These are the ones who clearly demonstrate their rage. They have a constant attitude of, "Don't cross my path or you will regret it!" They are the ones who blow up whenever, wherever. They simply vent at any time, using any words, with any attitude. They always have to be right, and nothing and no one can tell them otherwise.

Then there are those I like to call the "Internalisers". They are a bit dangerous to decipher because they don't show their feelings. You never know when they're unhappy with something you've done until it reaches a boiling point.

Neither of these is healthy in a marriage. We need to have an open line of communication to express our true feelings and keep each other happy.

> *"Let all bitterness, and wrath, and anger, and clamour, and evil speaking, be put away from you, with all malice:"* (Eph. 4:31)

All these ingredients need to be gotten rid of to control our anger and fear. Verse 32 goes on to explain how we need to be towards each other to successfully manage our emotions.

> *"And be ye kind one to another, tender-hearted, forgiving one another, even as God for Christ's sake hath forgiven you."*

When our heart is open to dealing with issues, we are in a better position to keep positivity in our marriages.

Earlier we mentioned that the Bible says you can be angry, but you should not sin. When your anger gets to the stage of being explosive, it becomes a sin. The Bible also states that you should not let the sun go down on your wrath. Whatever has gone wrong should not be allowed to linger but be dealt with as soon as possible. Otherwise, the enemy of our souls will bring other suggestions, for example: "You're not valued. That's why they speak to you like that." Be certain to put the devil in his place! *"Neither give place to the devil."* (Ephesians 4:27

This action of dealing with anger is so important to God that he gave us clear instructions about what should be done. It's God's will for us to show love in the face of these times.

> *And be ye kind one to another, tender-hearted, forgiving one another, even as God for Christ's sake hath forgiven you."* (Ephesians 4:32)

When unresolved anger begins to fuel resentment, unforgiveness, murmurings, etc., you have crossed the line to sinning. Take a step back, examine yourself and come back to God's guidelines.

What if the action that caused the anger cannot be resolved before the sun goes down? For instance, you might have caught your spouse in some immoral, unethical or majorly dishonest act. God understands that such matters cannot be resolved overnight. He created us after all, so He knows how deep our outrage and hurt will run, depending on the nature of the disappointment. If you must face such a situation, allow God to mould your heart and mind in **resolution seeking**, rather than **resentment sustaining**. Bear in mind that forgiveness can be INSTANT, but trust will need to be rebuilt.

Resolving Anger in Marriage

4 things we need to master:

1. Communicate subtly. This means we need to understand our spouse and know how to make the words we say effective. Here's a checklist you can pay attention to when doing this:

    a. Affirm your spouse before talking about your complaint, e.g. "Darling, I really love the way you (place thing here), but right now, I'm angry about (place issue here). This makes them see that you value them above whatever is making you uncomfortable and upset. You love them, but want to be able to speak with them honestly.

    b. When you lay out the complaint, don't criticise, thrash them with your words, lash out or vent. Do your best to be non-confrontational.

2. Practice immediate forgiveness before the issue gets out of hand. Yes, you're cross, and possibly rightfully so, but it's better to forgive sooner rather than later.

   "But God commendeth his love toward us, in that, while we were yet sinners, Christ died for us." (Rom. 5:8)

   The example here is that Christ died for us while we were still dirty with sin; He forgave us even before we accepted His gift of forgiveness. So, if your spouse has offended you and you go to communicate about it, do so with the same level of forgiveness that Christ showed to us. Forgiveness does not mean you won't acknowledge the issue, nor does it mean that you bottle up things and forget about whatever is troubling you. Forgiveness allows you to open up in a loving and forgiving way; to let go of the 'rage' before starting to deal with the matter, and to properly manage the conversation. Forgive so you can move on. Unforgiveness is like holding someone down

– you need to be in the same location (down) with them to keep them there. Forgiveness gives you the freedom to properly process what's happening.

It is important that your children have a positive view of how to resolve anger in marriage because they will mirror what they see.

3. Practice past forgiveness. Sometimes the indignation you feel may be unrelated to the present matter, it may be something based on a past event. Deal with the past, so it doesn't constantly crop up. Admit the root cause of the past problem or emotion, and allow the blood of Jesus to intervene. Past pent up emotions create barriers which make you defensive or accusatory at every little thing. If you have identified the event that created these feelings, pray about it or for the person involved. This helps to release them or it from that hold in your mind. Jesus encourages us to pray for and bless our enemies.

4. Recognise the triggers and deeply discuss them at length with your spouse. Is there a particular thing your spouse does which provokes you? Identify it and talk about the matter fully. Sometimes you may need counselling. Determine to seek help if necessary. There is no shame in saying you need support in dealing with the matter. Get the right kind of help.

Action Points:

1. Reflecting on the past, write down the positive and negative ways anger has been handled in your marriage.

2. Do you now know how you can practically apply information from this chapter to improve the way you both handle anger?

CHAPTER ELEVEN

5 reasons married couples should have sex regularly

Foundation: 1 Corinthians 7:3-5.

> *Let the husband render unto the wife due benevolence: and likewise also the wife unto the husband. The wife hath not power of her own body, but the husband: and likewise also the husband hath not power of his own body, but the wife. Defraud ye not one the other, except it be with consent for a time, that ye may give yourselves to fasting and prayer; and come together again, that Satan tempt you not for your incontinency.*

Sex is a very pleasurable thing designed by God to be enjoyed within the parameters of a marital relationship. It keeps the juices flowing and dynamics sharp. So, how often should a married couple have sex? Paul advises here that you should have it as often as possible unless there is an agreement between you to abstain for a pre-determined period. As soon as that period is over, couples should resume so that they don't drive each other to wandering temptation (looking elsewhere for sexual fulfilment).

However, most couples face the frustration of one partner having a consistently stronger sex drive than the other, which often leads to some levels of frustration on both sides. It's rare for both of you to be in the mood at the same time, but sex isn't always about personal satisfaction – whether you feel like it or not. It's about selflessness, sacrifice and meeting your partner's needs. Even if you're not in the mood, sex is pleasurable, so you'll most likely enjoy it.

Sex increases your intimacy level, your depth of communication and helps you connect with each other. I encourage you to make love as often as you can. Make it your goal not to deprive each other.

Dress to impress your spouse! Ladies, a man is moved by what he sees. If you were to examine marriages where the husband has strayed, the female third party is often well-dressed, with an exposed cleavage and fitted and/or short outfits. The wife, on the other hand, is typically overly modestly dressed.

Ladies be modest but attractive to your husband. Find out what he likes and wear that. If you don't feel comfortable wearing it outdoors, wear it at home. Make him happy! There are fewer restrictions on what to wear in your home than when you're out, so up your game! Get some fantastic lingerie and model it for him. Guys, get those silky or brand name boxers and flash them. Wear the vests and let her see your chest. Have fun with each other in the run up to and while having sex.

1. Frequent lovemaking will bring you and your spouse closer together on three levels:

    (a) Physically: Sex is the most pleasurable activity between a husband and wife. It has been shown that the endorphins released during the act generally make people happier. It also burns a lot of calories, so if you want to lose weight, have sex!

(b) Emotionally: Your heart is in it when you're relating to your spouse this way. You feel their love coming to you, and a deep connection arises and draws you closer to each other.

(c) Spiritually: After the pleasure comes contentment. When you pray later or even the next day, you can pray as one, because your hearts are bonded.

Couples need to discuss the topic of sex. You need to say what you do and don't like and tell each other what you want to explore. God gave it for enjoyment in marriage, so enjoy it to the fullest. Just like in any other area, your spouse is not a mind reader, so openly talk to them. Most Christians don't like discussing sex, so they bury the topic, or they go all shy, and then when they face sexual famine with their spouse, they don't know how to communicate to bring about change.

Church Ministers, this is for you too. We come to church all soberly dressed, sometimes us women we dress so straight. However, remember that your other half has eyes and a memory. They see all the other ladies and gentlemen who come to church dressed nicely, but modestly and these thoughts can linger! It has been proven that at some point during any marriage, the husband and the wife have both been attracted to someone else. Make sure you're talking about sex with your spouse. Let them know how often you want it, how you like it, what you want from it.

Affirm each other when you're doing it right! Men especially need to be admired during sex. When you can tell him, "yes, I like it like that", he ups his game because he loves that you love what he's doing. Your admiration really boosts his confidence. Acknowledge what's going on during your lovemaking because your sexual fulfilment is the cement of your marriage.

2. The more you make love with your spouse, the more potential it has to impact on your overall health and wellbeing. A healthy sex life within the parameters of marriage can lead to a healthy life overall.

3. Someone once said sex is only for procreation. This is a huge misconception! God created Adam and Eve naked and gave them desires for each other. Most marriages that use sex for procreation only tend not to last very long, because the party with the high sex drive feels deprived and is driven to look elsewhere for satisfaction. Sex is for pleasure as well as procreation. Don't deprive your spouse.

4. Research has shown that regular lovemaking between married couples (three to four times per week) could actually make you more successful in your career. As a man, you feel you can take on the whole world when you can conquer in the bedroom. When your wife meets your need, it shows she's behind you, supporting you. You can think better, analyse more creatively and it goes a long way to help you go the extra mile towards success. For women, a good sex life improves your confidence because you feel attractive and desired by your husband. There is nothing like a woman feeling desired. Your husband

can say "I love you" more times than you can count, but that feeling of being DESIRED, not just wanted, DESIRED, gives more inner power than most things. Our self-esteem is improved.

5. Regular and consistent sex can lower levels of stress and sexual frustration in your marriage, especially for men. They know they're coming home to an attractive wife who is prepared for them, and the bonding activity, particularly after dinner, helps to reduce the stress levels in their life.

6. Regular and consistent sex statistically lower the risks and temptations that can lead to adultery. It's like food. If you fill up at home with good food, you're not tempted by attractive-looking fast food which isn't good for your health. When you enjoy satisfying, fulfilling lovemaking in your home with your lovely wife or wonderful husband, you're not interested in anything outside, even if it's thrown at you.

A final word of encouragement: Remember, talk to your spouse about sex. Don't be quiet and hyper-spiritual at home, then when you're out, and hear some other person talking about it; you're positively shaking in your boots. NO! God gave you *this* spouse to have fun and enjoy a wonderful sex life. Discuss your sexual likes and dislikes, make time to have sex and be more fulfilled in this and other areas of your lives.

Action Points:

1. Discuss how the understanding you have both gained from this topic will help improve your sexual intimacy.

2. Set out how it will also affect and improve other areas of your marriage.

CHAPTER TWELVE

Communication and sex

Why do I have to talk about sex??

The first thing is, the more you communicate with your spouse, the more sexual you both become. Communication is a mega need for women, so the more you get into their world and talk things through, the more sexual she becomes.

In the last chapter, I mentioned that constant communication opens the man to his wife's world on three levels a) Physically, b) Emotionally, c) Spiritually. When we learn to communicate openly, particularly about sex, it unlocks the woman's world. It's almost like sex before sex. Talking lets you see your wife 'naked before you' in these three areas, and there's no better place to be. We encourage you to talk to her constantly and don't forget to listen.

In a marriage situation, what brings about physical, emotional and spiritual detachment between a husband and wife is secrecy brought on by a consistent lack of communication. Not talking to each other creates secrecy and kills intimacy. Faking it when your spouse touches you, won't last forever. It will eventually begin to affect everything else.

Secrets help evil to thrive while openness and communication allow a relationship to grow and develop. The Bible encourages us to walk in the light. Secrets are formed in the dark and need the darkness to stay alive. Communicate and bring those issues to light. Don't let dark things stop your marriage from being the light that it can be for you and others looking on.

Secrecy is the enemy of intimacy, but openness and honesty enhance sexual intimacy. Couples should communicate about everything and anything. On social media sites, you ought to know about each other's friends. Even if you don't know them personally, you should know of them. What does this have to do with sex? In today's electronic and social media driven world, any uncertainty or hidden worlds will begin to lead to, distrust, doubt, insecurity, and eventually the destruction of your marriage. Show your spouse that they are the most important person in your life—SHARE.

Non-verbal communication

Never use your body to punish your spouse. This is a form of nonverbal communication or passive aggression. You've missed the point if you do this.

> *Wives, be subject to your husbands [subordinate and adapt yourselves to them], as is right and fitting and your proper duty in the Lord. Husbands, love your wives [be affectionate and sympathetic with them] and do not be harsh or bitter or resentful toward them.* (Colossians 3: 18 AMPC)

If you've not seen this before, understand that really, once you're married, you've more or less agreed to 'sex on demand' with each other. Withholding your body as a means of punishment is telling your spouse you are rejecting them. No one likes to be rejected; especially not by the individual they've made a conscious decision to hold most dear i.e. your husband or wife.

TALK!

What would satisfy you sexually? This needs to be verbally communicated. Communication – speaking it out and listening – shows you are committed to meeting each other's needs. You may have an idea at the back of your mind regarding what you want to do to make your marriage work. Neither of you is a mind reader, so leaving the thought at the back of your mind will not help. You need to SAY, so that your spouse can operate in knowledge. They need to hear it.

Say what you like and what you DON'T like. Wives are free to communicate their sexual needs and should be free to do this without facing bias from their husbands. Men, do you realise that when your wife initiates sexual activity, you are even more aroused? The greatest satisfaction for a man is to know his wife wants him. Communicating in this way is the mature thing to do.

Can a husband or wife talk about their sexual past and still be accepted? Yes! They can and they should. Especially if there are lingering negative feelings resulting from past relationships. Talk about these things BEFORE you get married. If you are already married and haven't yet talked about them, make the earliest opportunity and get those feelings in the open. Deal with things maturely. The past is past, and neither person should be held to ransom over what they did.

You need to have a vision for your sex life that is discussed and committed to by both parties. Open communication also paves the way to reaching full climax for both husband and wife. Your sexual life gets better and better as you enact what your spouse has said they want and need. Make sex an open topic. If couples have a joint vision for sexual fulfilment, sex becomes more exciting and fulfilling. This is because you're entering the covenant with a clearer understanding of what is required to make it fun, successful and fully satisfying.

Boundaries

Never develop an inappropriate or emotional sexual relationship with another person, regardless of the condition of your marriage. There is the temptation to do this when things are tough or not going the way you expect them to. I'm not only talking about a physical relationship here but also connecting with someone else on an emotional level. Jesus said if you even look at someone that way in your heart, you've sinned.

It's very easy to develop these emotional attachments to people who give you attention where your spouse fails, possibly in the form of compliments, a listening ear, or maybe they make you their listening ear. These things make you feel valued and appreciated, and you may resent your spouse for not doing the same. Control your thoughts with WORDS. Speak out what you want to happen. There is significant power in speaking something out loud. Hearing it while you're speaking resonates in your spirit in a way thoughts cannot, so when the temptation arises, speak out against it in Jesus' name and remove yourself from it.

Communication during sex

Communication during sex isn't the easiest thing to decipher as sex is usually so pleasurable;

Communication and sex

communication isn't the first thing on your mind. However, this time of bonding is so essential to a married couple that communication during this time is intimate and important.

Men love to be verbally commended during the act. It brings them much satisfaction. Most husbands want to know that they are satisfying their wives during sex. Nothing cheapens a man's confidence more than when his wife verbalises that he can't perform. If he does something that makes you feel amazing, say so, and I mean, SAY so. Not just by making sounds like '...mmm'. Tell him what he's done and how it made you feel. Let him see your response. Express your pleasure with your body and words,' if you need to reiterate the point.

Women love to be physically admired and told about how attractive they are during sex. Tell your wife how attractive she is to you. Enumerate her physical attributes that get you going. Yes, men, you need to be verbal. This not only affirms her physical beauty to you but also your appreciation of who she is to you and an acknowledgement of what she does for your family.

Quickies have their place and can be handy, but sometimes for deeper connections, you need to take good time and enjoy the sex. Men and women connect during sex, and this cannot really be achieved without communicating before and during the act. It doesn't help to just jump on the bed, groan a few times, and then it's all over (at least for one of you), and you fall asleep.

Turn on your bedroom voice and caress your spouse's ears. Put the non-sexual touches in place, knowing once you do this, the mood is being set, and intimacy will most likely follow. Both spouses love each other's responsiveness during sex. Don't just talk with actions or sounds, use words.

Men love their wives initiating sex. It arouses them greatly. In today's world, we've made women feel like they are 'forward' for being the initiators and that it's their place to be pursued. However, in the context of marriage, there's absolutely nothing wrong with a wife initiating sexual activity. There are things you could do to let him know you're in the mood – using your body by either stroking your thigh or some other part of your body, for example.

Or it may be that look in your eye. Sometimes, just say, "Hey babe, I want you!" There's no mistaking what you want when you're direct, is there? Ladies, initiate away!

Romance. This shows that you are on each other's minds. Show it throughout the day. A text, a call, a picture can make all the difference to how the evening is enjoyed. Wives love the romance of a phone call, a loving word or anything that affirms her and displays how you feel about her.

There's a world of pleasure just waiting for you to enjoy as husband and wife. Talk about what you want and put it into action.

Action Points:

1. Intentionally engage in a week or two of talking deeply to each other about sex and during sex.

2. At the end of this period, write down how your relationship has been affected and plan practical ways to make this a permanent feature in your marriage.

CHAPTER THIRTEEN

Your money, My money – Our money

Partly adapted from *'Money Crashers – 18 money management tips for married couples'*, by Casey Slide[1].

Whether we like it or not, money plays a vital role in marriage and is one of the key areas you need to get right. If a couple can get the money dynamic right, other things will fall into place. During our years of counselling, we've found that couples often don't take the time to talk about money, so we decided to address this. Let's start at the beginning.

When you get married, money stops being 'mine' and becomes 'ours'. You're both working hard to make sure the family is well taken care of, so you should come together to plan your financial goals.

---

1 (Slide, 2017 (Updated))

Part of the marital vows made in church is: "for better, for worse, for richer, for poorer". Obviously, you become richer if you have more money and poorer if you have less money, so, let's look at how you can maximise the opportunities you have as husband and wife, and the favour you can enjoy from God when you plan together.

As the saying goes: "he who fails to plan, plans to fail". A husband and wife must plan to agree on money matters. How you grew up handling money may differ, and you may find that one spouse loves to spend while the other loves to save. You now need to agree on a compromise regarding how your money will be jointly handled. If this isn't done, there will be a higher occurrence of friction in your home. So how do you balance this to make both of you happy?

Scriptural basis

> *Every kingdom split up against itself is doomed and brought to desolation, and so house falls upon house. [The disunited household will collapse.]* Luke 11: 17b AMPC

The Bible encourages husbands and wives to cleave to each other and become one. When disagreements regarding money occur, it's like a kingdom divided against itself – it will fall.

> *Do two walk together except they make an appointment and have agreed?* (Amos 3:3 AMPC)

We can only walk together in agreement.

> *Where there is no vision [no redemptive revelation of God], the people perish;* (Prov. 29:18a AMPC)

Remember you are now in a home with children (or they will be coming along) so your financial vision will impact generations to come. If there is no vision for managing money, there will be suffering.

A few things need to be done as a couple where managing finances are concerned.

1. **Never shy away from talking about finances.** Ideally, both parties should discuss this before marriage, but if you haven't, please start immediately. Money management goes a long way to ensuring a successful home.

If you were wondering who should be the provider, according to the Bible, it is the man. The Bible says in 1 Timothy 5:8, *But if any provide not for his own, and specially for those of his own house, he hath denied the faith, and is worse than an infidel.*

It is a husband's responsibility to take care of, work, and provide for his family.

When a godly man does his best but is down on finances, he is not very happy and feels unable to provide for his family as much as he ought to. His family may not view it that way, but he, recognising the structure God put in place, will get these feelings. We live in contemporary times, however, and there's nothing wrong with the wife helping out financially.

2. **Write down monetary goals.** Discuss your long-term financial goals in depth. You may be a young couple now, but there's nothing wrong with discussing the age at which you hope to retire and what you plan to have

saved or invested towards that. If you want to become millionaires (regardless of the currency), talk about what you're going to do to get there. If you're in debt, you also need to plan how to get out of it so you can start making meaningful progress in your lives.

Out of these plans, budgeting comes into place. You'll need to agree on a current level of spending, and stick to it. This means before you leave the house to go shopping, have a predetermined amount to spend and abide by that. No more going into the shop for specific items, only to see something else and think, *well, this one thing won't break the budget,"* so you pick it up. Then the same happens with several items, and by the time you're done, your trolley is full, and you've smashed the budget. Things like this happen when there's no focus, and you haven't bought into goal setting or budgeting. You do not need to buy everything you set eyes on, just because you can.

3. **Assess your accounts and plan how to make them better.** Look at all bank and savings accounts, as well as your debts, including credit cards, store cards, bank and other loans. This way you are both clear on the grounds on which to proceed.

You can have individual accounts and joint accounts. I have my own account, Ishola has his and we have a joint one. So that's my money, his money and our money. Now, having my own account does not mean 'my money' is not his money or vice versa. When we have payments to come in which are delayed, but some bills for which Ishola is responsible become due, I transfer the money into his account if I have enough to cover it, and when he gets it back, he repays me. We have that kind of agreement between us. There's no room for, 'Oh, I don't want to touch my money! You'll have to ask for an extension on a repayment date. The money is OURS, regardless of which account it's in. It's important that <u>financial independence</u> does not make <u>financial interdependence</u> suffer. If you don't like the idea of joint accounts, that's fine, but be transparent with what you have!

4. **Build an emergency fund** as much as you can. The fact that you have a fantastic job now doesn't mean that you are secure. I remember when the recession hit in 2008, lots of people who had secure jobs lost them. Also, during the recent oil crisis, many people who worked in this sector lost their jobs. Those who were not wise enough to have investments and savings jumped from pillar to post to find any job, just to keep body and soul together. You must have an emergency fund where you both put money away just in case. If there comes a time when there's no income, then you can turn to what you've put aside.

As Christians, we use the **70:20:10** rule. 10% is a tithe of what you earn which you give to your local assembly, the Kingdom and the work of the ministry; 20% goes to your savings, and 70% is what you use to cover the household expenses. If this is done constructively, over time, you will have some savings. This, in turn, can help you through hardship, or provide a source for investing in other projects which can bring in more income. Nothing stops a husband and wife from having multiple streams of income; in fact, we encourage you to work towards this. Don't depend on one source of income.

5. **Track your budget.** See if you need to realign or revisit it. We recommend that you have weekly money meetings to see how you're doing with the budget and what needs to be changed or maintained. It can be hard for the husband to have these meetings, especially if he's doing his best and the funds aren't coming in as expected. You should still have the meeting; discuss what has happened and what you're going to do to follow up. Women love to hear this. Men tend to feel that there is shame attached to talking about their lack of money and they withdraw. Remember that women are looking for you to lead the home, so have the meeting, talk and plan honestly.

6. **Start to plan and save for your retirement.** If you are a part of the national pension fund, that's great, however, if you can afford more, have a personal pension fund. This will be beneficial for your family. The Bible says a righteous man leaves an inheritance for his children's children. Think in generational terms - both material and spiritual. Ask yourself, "If I died today, what am I leaving for them?"

7. **If you're both in debt, the plan should be to get out and stay out of debt.** This situation can put a strain on your relationship. The debt may be the husband's or the wife's, but now that you're married, you need to plan to get out of it TOGETHER. It's now 'OUR DEBT'.

Other money management tips for the husband and wife:

1. Share responsibilities. This demonstrates that you're a team and that the burden rests on both of you. The husband may be the main provider, but there are some responsibilities

that can rest on the wife. The husband feels the value of the wife in the home when she's able to partake of that responsibility, no matter how tiny or how little it might be. Sharing helps with communication and intimacy.

2. If you've gotten into a sticky financial situation, approach touchy subjects with love. e.g., if your spouse invests family money, but then loses it all. How do you handle that? They would know they've made a mistake, or they've been cheated out of business. These things happen, and they realise it. However, if you are taunting them at home with statements like: "Look what you've done!" or "See the trouble you've put us in!" or even, "this has nothing to do with me. You sort it out." this is the wrong approach. Don't do anything rash that might damage the relationship. Bring up money subjects with care and love. Imagine, if the investment had worked, you would have been over the moon! Bear in mind that a loss today does not mean a loss forever. You can get back up again.

If you feel your spouse is overspending, don't start yelling and making accusations. Lovingly bring up the fact that they've overspent that month or week, and look at ways to bring it back into budgeted alignment. Always view yourself as a team, not as individuals who happen to be together.

3. Decide on the right level of investment risk. Investments are risky, but discuss what levels you're both comfortable with and step out in faith, trusting God for the increase. Remember that both of you need to take responsibility for the outcome. Ask yourselves, "What steps can we take to expand the financial base of this family?" These things need to be agreed between you.

4. Work as a team. When you do this, you become aware of each other's strengths and weaknesses. This way you synergise to succeed.

5. BE HONEST!! No one should be doing anything with money that the other is not

aware of. I heard the story of a couple who lived as though they were in abject poverty. The wife stayed home to look after the family while the husband went out to work. She trusted him with money matters and managed the house according to the financial status he told her they were in. So, she dressed, shopped and cooked as though they were poor. One day, while looking through their mail, as usual, she opened an envelope addressed to her husband and found a bank statement showing there were hundreds of thousands of dollars in the account! When she saw this, she almost passed out! She immediately filed for divorce because he had not been honest. When asked why he did this, the husband said he was afraid they were going to become poor, and he didn't want to ever not have money put away, so he never told her. Being open about money from the onset can prevent problems.

6. Trust your spouse. If there is deceit, trust cannot exist. The dishonest spouse will always

be accused of hiding something – even when they are being completely honest.

7. Learn from each other. No one is a total expert, and no one knows everything. Both of you will make some money mistakes but learn from them so you can make money successes.

8. Give 100% of yourselves to money matters that concern both of you and the family. Careful and wise planning and budgeting should be done as a couple, not individually.

9. Remember your vows. For richer, or for poorer. No one expects to be poorer, but if the economy changes or investments don't go to plan, remember your vows. Bear in mind that no situation is permanent – things can change at any time.

Question: If the man trying hard to provide is struggling to cope, is he of less worth to his wife?

Answer: That should never be the case. A woman should not value her man any less if he is doing his best to provide for the family. If her income can supplement what he is earning, they should work together to manage the household. When we first got married, I was earning double my husband's wages. If we wanted to, let's say, buy a TV, if he could put in £200 from his income, I would contribute the other £600. My husband was STILL THE PROVIDER. I only supplemented. The man should be able to contribute a proportion of his earnings. Many husbands take their wives' earning power for granted and won't take responsibility, which can be frustrating for the woman. This is sad. No matter what you earn as a man, you are the PROVIDER.

I personally believe you still need to give your wife some spending or pocket money, no matter how little it is. It's the thought that counts. It makes her feel you are not taking her position as your helpmeet for granted. Some women wouldn't bother jointly contributing—they don't care—but the woman who really loves her husband will take on some responsibility, especially when the husband does not have that much money available. There is nothing wrong with a woman sharing responsibility for the bills. The Proverbs 31 woman is the kind of wife any husband wants. On the other hand, there is something wrong with a man intentionally depending on his wife to pay the bills.

Action Points:

1. What insight(s) have you gained from this chapter?

2. Moving forward, how will what you have learned improve the way you both deal with finances?

CHAPTER FOURTEEN

Six financial mistakes couples make

Talk without action won't take you anywhere, but you *can* take the wrong approach! As you plan financially, watch out for these pitfalls and ensure you avoid and/or overcome them.

- Merging your finances - deciding whether you should have a joint account or not. WRONG approach: saying to your spouse, "United we stand but divided we bank." Each spouse should know what's in the other's bank account. Remember, it's yours, mine and ours.

- Dealing with debt. WRONG approach: One person is blamed for and given the responsibility to fix your debt. Nagging comments like: "it's not my business" and "I didn't ask you to go and do this or that" are completely wrong. You are in this together.

It's our debt, let's decide how to pay it off.

- Keep spending in check. WRONG approach: saying to your spouse "I'm a saver, you're the spender. That is our problem! It's why we don't have any money." The truth is you both spend but on different things. It's better to say, "Ok, our priorities may be a bit different, so let's budget."

- Investing wisely. Some men are risk takers. They always feel their financial investments will turn around and make their lives much better. WRONG approach: "You're a risk taker, I'm a risk avoider. Hands off our savings, hands off our pension and don't go near what I've managed to put aside." The right approach is to think in time frames and take as much time as your goals allow. Instead of making a large investment, start small and see how it goes, then gradually scale up.

Keeping money secrets. What your spouse doesn't know can't hurt him or her? The truth could hurt

Six financial mistakes couples make

them when they find out, and moreover, big financial secrets can ruin a marriage.

- Emergency planning. WRONG approach: "We're fine; we don't need to worry about money." So you don't have any backup financial plan, no insurance or savings in place. Think about the children. The right approach is to accept that anything can happen, so you need to plan for emergencies.

Action Point:

1. What practical steps can you both take to avoid financial mistakes in your marriage?

CHAPTER FIFTEEN

How to pray for your spouse

This is not one of the ingredients mentioned in chapter two, but I encourage you to pray for your marriage like it is a physical entity. It holds such importance in Christian marriage that I decided to dedicate an entire chapter to this topic.

Not only should you pray for your marriage, but take the time to specifically pray for your spouse. Pray for God's will and purpose to be fulfilled in your marriage. Never stop praying - it works! God answers prayer. Asking for your marriage to excel and prosper, for love to increase, for God's blessing and for financial open doors are all good things. Pray for them.

Your marriage is filled with purpose and destiny. It is a living example of "Thus saith the Lord". Your relationship should model God's ideal for marriage as a prophetic voice to this generation. It should reflect the relationship between Christ and His bride—the Church. She was not perfect before he chose to die for her, and even now, He washes and cleanses her to present her blameless before God. This right here is the PRIMARY purpose of marriage—to demonstrate God's Kingdom agenda here on earth, and should be the principal reason for YOUR marriage. If it is placed first, the secondary purposes—companionship, sexual enjoyment, fruitfulness, security, and so on, will all be achieved. Even when these are yet to materialise, you are able to stay focused on the primary purpose while still enjoying your marriage rather than enduring it!

Here are **5 suggestions on how to pray specifically for your spouse**.

1. Pray for your spouse's spouse – THAT'S YOU! Someone said some time ago the most popular prayer spouses pray is for God to change the other person. Sometimes we need to look inward and ask God to change us. Your heart must be clean before God before you start praying

since it's not possible to pray in truth for someone you're angry with. Situations occur here and there in marriage, which can make you unhappy with your spouse every day; however, we *are* called to pray <u>daily</u>.

Be honest about your feelings so you'll be able to pray effectively. Tell God how you feel, but then ask Him to take away the hurt, pain, disappointment, release you from anger, and allow His forgiveness to flow. You'll see the vast difference it makes to your prayers and the answers you receive. If you put on the armour of prayer, you can achieve far more than if you were to implement all the other great things mentioned in this book without prayer. Pray without ceasing for your spouse, whether you feel like it or not.

2. Pray for your spouse's relationship with God. You need to be able to pray that your spouse will <u>Know God, Trust God and Remain in God</u>. We could take many of the

things we allow ourselves to be confronted with to God and let Him deal with them. God is THE ENFORCER. Regardless of what you want to see in your spouse; if you try to be the enforcer, all you'll get are roadblocks. On the other hand, it's difficult to stay offended when you're praying for someone.

3. John 15:5 & 7 says:

I am the vine, you are the branches. He who abides in Me, and I in him, bears much fruit; for without Me, you can do nothing… If you abide in Me, and My words abide in you, you will ask what you desire, and it shall be done for you.

Without Jesus, your spouse can't be patient, love you unconditionally, or be the person you desire them to be. The closer your spouse is to God the better they will treat you, and know how to handle things in your home. So, before you lay down a never-ending "honey-do" list, remember to pray before you say.

How to pray for your spouse

When we spend time praying, God takes away our natural fleshly selves and replaces it with His attributes.

4. Pray for your spouse's God-given role in the marriage. Determine what each person's role is. What should you, the wife, be praying for regarding your husband? His role as the man, leader and initiator in your home. You can write down your own personal confessions to speak over him. This should be determined on a phase by phase basis since we do life in seasons. In addition to the personal confessions you have specifically crafted for him, ask God to give him the strength to carry out his responsibilities and prioritise time with his family. The Lord has entrusted money, time and a home to you. Pray for wisdom to be good stewards of what He's blessed you with.

Husbands, pray for your wife's role as your partner, wife and help meet. Ask God to remind her to pray about her worries so she can experience God's peace. Pray that her day will go smoothly and that she will accomplish much. It's important to pray for each other's roles so that we can effectively function in them. Pray that your spouse's heart will be safely entrusted with you.

5. Pray for strong relationships with godly members of the same sex. Same-sex friendships are vital. If a person looks to their spouse alone to meet all their friendship needs, chances are, the spouse will crumble under the pressure. Remember that your spouse will have people of the same sex that they spend time with who will influence them. If you want to know your influencers, make a list of your top three friends. Those are the people affecting the way you think and do things. You'll need to pray about your influencers, as you need to have various levels of friendships. It's lethal to have the wrong friendships and influencers. Someone who's not married or experienced

How to pray for your spouse

enough in life may not be the best person to advise you about situations you may face. Men, you also need to think about *marriage mentorship*. You may need to consult with your elders from time to time to gain from their wisdom. The term 'elders' is **not** based on age. Jesus was thirty-three, and much younger than many people he encountered, but he was a man of wisdom and therefore counted as an elder.

6. Pray practically. Some people may be quite busy and find it difficult to pinpoint a specific time or place to pray. In this case, you can pray on the go, but you need to have a plan. Choose Scriptures that relate to praying for your spouse. Make a list of areas you want to pray specifically for and write down those confessions. This enables you to cover them in prayer when you have a quiet moment at work, while you're doing the laundry, at the gym or on your commute to work. You can pray out loud or in your heart.

Let me give you an example. I know of a lady in Nigeria who prayed over her husband's photograph. While he was out to work, she would make practical confessions over that photo, calling him a man of influence who would be positively remembered for generations to come.

Speak not just to your spouse's future, but to things that they need right now – their priorities or frustrations; what's angering or upsetting them. Pray over those things. The confession of your marital vows before God makes you one in spirit, so when you stand in the gap for your spouse, it creates an express road to the Throne and God intervenes. Pray your spouse into their destiny in God and in life.

Remember, your spouse is God's gift to you. You didn't just pick them up along the way, or from a street corner somewhere, somehow. God enabled, in fact, predestined them to come into your path, for you to meet and be together. That means they have a purpose and reason for being in your life. They're there, not to bring you down, but to build you up. Proverbs 10: 22 tells us that *the blessing of the LORD, it maketh rich, and He addeth no sorrow with it.*

The issues you may be facing are not to bring sorrow, but God wants you to be strong and find a way to work out your differences so your marriage can be the blessing it's designed to be. Then He can give wealth, prosperity, fruitfulness, joy and stability in every area of your life.

When praying for your spouse, you have access to God through Christ. The Bible says God hears us whenever we pray in Jesus' name (Jn. 14:13-14; 16:23), and that means he receives our petition. Furthermore, it says you should believe that you have received whatever you ask for in faith, and you will have it. (Mk. 11:24)

God has the final say about things that happen, but understand that you can influence Him as you pray for your marriage. The example of Psalm 1:1–3 shows a character that can command the heavens and have them.

> *Blessed is the man that walketh not in the counsel of the ungodly, nor standeth in the way of sinners, nor sitteth in the seat of the scornful. But his delight is in the law of the LORD; AND IN HIS LAW DOTH HE MEDITATE DAY AND NIGHT. And he shall be like a tree planted by the rivers of water, that bringeth forth his fruit in his season; his leaf also shall not wither; and whatsoever he doeth shall prosper.*

We can pray and receive things from the Lord when we walk in His way and pray according to His will for us. Your marriage is work; you work your marriage to make it work. This is all about doing – *whatsoever he does shall prosper.*

Action Points:

1. What have you learned about praying for your spouse from this chapter?

2. Considering your busyness, what is the most suitable time you can dedicate to praying for your spouse?

3. Write down and commit to this time, protecting it from any invasion of work.

CHAPTER SIXTEEN

Honest advice from married couples

Married for 25 years

We met at Bible School in the Philippines where I was a 2nd-year student, and my now wife was the teacher. We got married and formed a multicultural, multiracial marriage. THEN we started to realise our differences, one of which was cultural. We had to find a way to work out peaceful Christ-centred resolutions using His wisdom. We needed to agree on the direction and the values we wanted to keep in our marriage. When we passed the ten-year milestone, it was good, but by the time you hit 20 years, you know you've passed most of the rocky roads. Never say you've arrived, though! You're always learning and cultivating that relationship.

We once visited a friend with a 37-year-old Rosebush. She was showing us how she looked after it and maintained its appearance so that it was ready to bloom for another season. We realised that marriages are a bit like that, they need to be cultivated and looked after in order to bloom in their season.

After being missionaries in the Philippines for almost 20 years, we moved to England. This was a real test of our marriage. Just as it was difficult for me to adjust in the Philippines, it was more difficult for her to adjust here, so we went to see our pastor.

"What attracted you to each other in the first place?" He asked.

"Our friendship." We said.

On hearing that, he recommended that we return to what brought us together.

Friendship transcends culture. Jesus calls us friends as well, doesn't He? When you cultivate friendship, it bears fruit. When we work on the areas in marriage that make us friends, it helps in the other areas, and we have something to draw on during difficult times.

Honest advice from married couples

Not cultivating friendship is like having a bank account but not making deposits. There's nothing to draw on or draw out when you have an emergency. There's no such thing as a friendship/relationship overdraft.

We discovered things we both liked to do which nourished the marriage, and we did and still do those things together. Yes, we have separate activities, but we make time for things we do together.

Our relationship with God is really what has kept our marriage together. While there is no certainty in this world, Christians have the only sure foundation in Jesus Christ. If our relationship with Him is secure, other relationships we have founded on him will be the same. Sometimes, when we really struggled in particular areas, we would be honest with God and ask for his help. Whenever we did that, we felt him give practical wisdom to nourish the soil of our marriage, and when I acted on the answer God gave me, the outcome affected my wife as well.

Remember, the Bible says that it's the little foxes that spoil the vine (Song of Solomon 2:15). It's usually the little irritating things become big unnecessary challenges.

We advise you to continually pray for each other. Also, rebuke the enemy whenever he is at work in your marriage, but not to your spouse's face. Our enemy is never our husband or wife. Apparently, what my wife does is to go into a cupboard where she screams at and rebukes the enemy. It's important to recognise the spirit behind the action. We have one enemy, and that is the devil.

Question: What is the biggest challenge you've faced in your 25 years and how did you manage it?

She says: The hardest thing is that I'm old fashioned. I always believed that marriage covenant shouldn't be broken, but things can go wrong and, if you're not careful, your emotions can really decide your future.

I once packed my bags and said,

"That's it, I'm done! God will forgive and give me another chance. I've seen other broken marriages restored or they've gone on to meet someone else."

Then God reminded me that He had told me this man was the one for me. This was after I had been engaged to someone else.

So, I asked myself the question: "Would I be able to live without this man?" I realised I couldn't because he is the one God gave to complete me, so I returned home. Now, when anything brings pain in our relationship, I go back to the Lord and ask Him how to deal with it. There are also times I wait until he's sleeping and lay hands on him. See, I'm a late-night person, and he's an early riser, so when we go to bed, he quickly falls asleep. That allows me the opportunity to sneakily lay hands on him and pray. Ladies, do whatever you can to preserve your marriage.

He says: There was a period after we moved back to the UK when our marriage began to drift and we started to enjoy doing things separately. We were living together but doing our own thing, which was dangerous. We eventually went for counselling, and the first thing our pastor asked me was, "Is there anyone else in the marriage?"

We confirmed that there wasn't, but we felt that our drifting apart had led us to wonder whether there was any hope for us.

Then our Pastor asked, "What brought you together in the first place? What did you do together that nourished your friendship?"

We realised it was going on days out. We've gone back to that and seen the benefit of spending our time together.

Couples need to guard their time together. When you feel yourself drifting apart, don't leave it or go confiding in someone else. Deal with it, or you may run into the danger zone of a third or even a fourth party in your marriage. That's when you've almost reached the point of destruction, which is not God's plan. Whatever you did to get to the happiness you're enjoying now is what you should continue doing to keep enjoying the relationship. All couples are different, so seek God for the wisdom needed for various challenges. When we come to difficult times, we have the reservoir of good times and agreements that we can draw on as we maturely discuss our disagreements. We also don't have to agree on everything, we can agree to disagree.

Give room for God's supernatural power

When we were drifting apart, my wife and I decided to go away for a weekend. We went to separate locations and didn't tell each other where we were going. She simply said she was going to seek the Lord. The children knew where she was, but I didn't. We didn't communicate with each other during that weekend, either. However, she kept listening to a specific song and, as God would have it, He used the same song to melt my heart as well.

This is the supernatural power of God working to keep your marriage together. When we were reconciled we compared notes and realised the song was *Surrender* by Hillsong.

Always give room for the supernatural power of God. We walk in obedience to what the Holy Spirit shows us by faith, but our faith in God will bring the results.

Forgiveness

We agree that forgiveness is the most important part of marriage. Without it, you cannot move forward. And it needs to be constant. Even if you forgave a minute ago, forgive again right now. Unforgiveness is like drinking poison and hoping the other person will die. Forgiveness frees you and keeps your marriage alive. Verbalise it so that you validate your decision to forgive.

Married for 10 years

My previous marriage lasted only three and a half years simply because I brought a lot of baggage from my past into it. However, as they say, if you want to change, do things differently to achieve the desired result. Below are some lessons I have learnt in marriage.

1. Deal with emotional baggage from childhood or previous relationships.

2. Overlook weakness, do not dwell on it. Find innovative ways to help your partner.

Honest advice from married couples

3. When there is a disagreement, find a win/win solution.

4. Do not try to win an argument; you may lose your relationship.

5. Celebrate your partner's strengths.

6. Pray for each other.

7. Make God the centre of your relationship.

8. Remind yourself often how God brought you together.

9. Make yourselves accountable to someone you respect, possibly an elder in the family.

10. Be clear about your roles and responsibilities in your family structure (1 Peter 3:1-9, Ephesians 5:21-27).

11. Make your partner secure in your relationship by being faithful in your marriage (Hebrews 13:4).

12. Learn to say sorry. I struggle with this all the time, but it goes a long way towards diffusing a conflict.

13. Do not get too many people involved in your business.

14. Protect your partner from your family.

15. Avoid using negative words. You cannot take them back once you have spoken them.

16. Know your partner's love language.

Married for 8 years

Expectations

We were still dating, and at the end of one phone call, I signed off with 'I miss you.' Of course, I waited to hear it echo down the line. All I got was a rather terse 'Goodnight.'

Naturally, I felt it was my duty to educate my soon-to-be husband on telephone etiquette, so I told him what he was meant to say at such a time. Instead, *I* got an education! He said *at that moment* he didn't *feel* like he was missing me, and he wasn't going to say something that wasn't true just because 'it was the thing to do.'

"Ok, I get it. Goodnight."

"Goodnight."

To be honest, I didn't get it. *Was I about to marry a man who didn't know how to be romantic or say the things I wanted to hear when I wanted to hear them? Could I live with that?*

It took a few hours, but when I considered all the other things about him that were just spot on, I realised I could live with it. That single moment of education alerted me to the existence of certain expectations I had of any man I married, which were not necessarily going to be met in the man I did marry. So, what did I do?

I started letting go of who I wanted him to be and began to appreciate and treasure just who he was.

What about him? Eight years on, my husband has discovered that, domestic goddess, I am not. I can just about do what needs to be done. He, on the other hand, loves to wash, clean, tidy, and arrange everything. Did I meet his expectations in that area? I doubt it! But God bless him, he dropped those expectations. He took me as I *am*, not as he wants me to be, and got me a dishwasher!

I believe accepting each other really makes us work. It has saved us from disappointment, frustration and resentment. We can even laugh about those shortcomings now. We both know that the laundry might not get folded away for a few days, so when I do get around to it earlier than usual, I get a smiling, 'Well done!" We both know that I shouldn't hold my breath waiting for a heart to heart speech on the depth of his feelings for me, the dishwasher already says it.

Some unmet expectations, if discovered before marriage, might be a deal breaker, but after getting married, they become issues you must deal with or simply let go. Are those expectations really important? Where have they even come from? Family history? Romance books? Hollywood? Other peoples' expectations? Martha and Mary can help with this (Lk 10:38-42): don't be too concerned with unnecessary things. Find what's truly important and don't let it go.

Married for 8 years

As a couple who has been married for 8 years, we have experienced several highs and lows of marriage. We have always believed our foundation was solid because we believe God brought us together. Both of us also had the same vision, based and focused on the kingdom of God, for our life and marriage. This did not mean it was always going to be a bed of roses or breakfast in bed kind of relationship. There was a lot to be done to make this marriage work and be enjoyable as we fulfilled God's purpose.

One of the first lessons we learned was to respect each other's opinions and feelings, and speak to and treat each other with grace. For instance, being the man or leader of the family did not mean the husband always had to be right, controlling or manipulative. We have both learnt that the husband needs to be **in control** of a home rather than **controlling** it. Being in control is more about managing the personalities in your home, understanding the periods and times they are going through, and dealing with them in line with God's word; while being controlling is wanting everyone to do what *you* want and reacting negatively when they don't. We have also learnt that being a wife means trusting your husband to lead the family even when it doesn't make sense, rather than taking laws into your hands.

We also used to do a whole lot of arguing which is common in marriages. We have since come to understand that the underpinning factor was a desire to win and have the last say. This was a major issue with us and presented a gaping hole for the devil to come into our marriage, which led to our keeping malice for days and cancelling family commitments. We and people around us suffered a lot from this. Looking back now, we feel all that arguing was an excuse to avoid being responsible and accountable.

Arguments lead to lawlessness and disorderliness and bring about a dysfunctional home. Once we identified the cause of most of our disagreements, which was the major source of unhappiness and destruction of our marriage, we decided to take some steps to ensure that the devil does not have his way in our union any longer. We have since become closer to one another as we realised that having separate agendas would get us nowhere near God's objectives for our lives. We had no choice but to accept each other for who we were, love and submit to each other and trust God to perfect us because it is in both our interests to become one.

Apart from the above points, some other things have worked for us.

1. Agreeing on how we are going to live our lives; what is acceptable and what is not. These are strictly based on the word of God which is our foundation (Can two walk together except they agree?)

2. Set boundaries to protect us and the marriage

3. Working at being each other's best friend.

4. Constantly doing a heart check-up, i.e., judging our motives

5. Abstaining from relationships that are unproductive or do not bring glory to God

6. Being open and honest with one another

7. Having a God-fearing mentor

Above all, one significant thing that has helped us through our marriage is our individual commitment to God. When you put God before your spouse and anything else, He will, in turn, put you and all that concerns you first.

Married for 5 Years

We met online (on a dating website) in 2010. Neither of us initially took it that seriously, but we exchanged emails, met up and were engaged within 3 months! We got married in 2012, and we often joke that it seems much longer than 5 years based on how many major life events happened within that time:

1. The death of our first-born son.

2. The birth of our daughter - our 'miracle of Jehovah' and 'Answered Prayer' (the meaning of her first and middle names).

3. Mental health issues.

4. Immigration problems.

Through it all, the first lesson we learned is that God is always present in every circumstance, and He's the only person we could truly rely on.

We learned the art of give and take/compromise, as when we each insisted on our own way it led to lots of arguments.

Being grateful for each other and every day we have together.

Being in a multicultural and multi-racial marriage; we have to negotiate differences. Edith recently reminded me of the first Christmas we shared with my family. It was totally unlike anything she had experienced before, and she felt it was boring. That was hard at the time for both of us, but we have gradually learnt to adjust and adapt. We are also trying to raise our daughter according to both cultures.

What we have also learnt over the past five years is love and respect for our Pastors at Rock Church. We saw how devastated Pastor Ishola was when Caleb died and how he was with us every step of the way - thinking about it still really moves me. Pastor Doris was amazing in supporting my wife during that time as well.

We are really blessed by the marriage ministry being developed at Rock Church and thank God for the large-scale effect it is having on so many around the world.

Our encouragement to married couples is to ensure you are both part of a local vibrant church family where you are deeply connected to God and submitted to spiritual authority. It definitely adds to the health of your marriage.

Married for 4 years

Before I started driving, I used to think the driver in a moving vehicle had their feet constantly on the accelerator. I soon realised there are times they're not on the accelerator at all. They need to apply the brakes, change gears, etc., while the vehicle is in motion.

Just like a vehicle in motion, every marriage experiences numerous challenges and circumstances to keep it moving. What matters is that you handle or deal with the different situations instead of shying away. Challenges in marriage should be seen as opportunities rather than obstacles. The focus in every marriage should be how to handle common and unique situations in order to further the marriage.

Just like faith without works is dead, a successful marriage requires both sides of the coin; God and personal commitment.

God and commitment

I've come to learn that it's not love that sustains a marriage, but commitment. Love, as we define it today, is simply infatuation or sexual feelings, and those are fickle. True love requires a high volume of sacrifice and selflessness. Many times, this can be very painful or make an individual feel like they are being taken advantage of, but if you prayerfully continue doing what is right, with the help of God; your spouse will come around to being who they need to be.

We often make the mistake of reciprocating evil for evil, but the Bible encourages us to repay evil with good. So, in any relationship where one spouse is a bit difficult, if the other continues prayerfully, patiently (sometimes painfully) the difficult one will come around. Remember the Bible says not to be weary in well doing because in due season we'll reap if we faint not (Gal 6:9).

Divorce is not an option

Many divorcees state "irreconcilable differences" as the reason for their breakup. No one is perfect; however, most of us will not break up with our siblings or children due to irreconcilable differences. Rather, we work through them and stay close because we consider them our blood or family.

Your spouse should be more to you than blood relations; more than a friend that sticks closer than a brother. As such, you need to work through all obstacles and challenges, including sexual infidelity (provided your spouse is not a habitual cheat who takes advantage of your willingness to forgive. Even the Bible says, "Shall we continue in sin that grace might abound? God forbid!" Rom. 6:1-2)

Other lessons include:

- Never try to change your spouse

- Never stop learning from and about each other

- One model doesn't fit all - don't copy, instead, find out what works for you

- Be intentional and prayerful about making your marriage a success

Married for 4 Years

My experience of marriage so far...

I was born into a Christian family and have been fervent but not perfect all my life. The youngest of my mother's children, I am a graduate and postgraduate degree holder; exposed to other cultures and people from different walks of life through studying abroad and travelling extensively when I was still single.

I eventually decided to take things further by prayerfully searching for the "right life partner", trusting God, and of course, "working the walk", since prayer won't do the talking and dinner dates for you!

James 2:14 says, *what doth it profit, my brethren, though a man say he hath faith, and have not works? Can faith save him?* Verse 17 adds, ... *Even so, faith, if it has no works, is dead, being alone* and then the popular verse 26 says… *for as the body without the spirit is dead, so faith without works is dead also…*

So I got busy with the "search for a life partner" work by myself. I wasn't confused at any point. Being a meticulous, finicky and over-particular kind of guy, I had already programmed all the qualities I wanted in a spouse into my mind. I wasn't going to compromise as I believe strongly that standards and practices should not only be maintained but improved upon!

Honest advice from married couples

To cut the epistle short, I entered my marriage with this mindset, but Mr Reality soon came knocking. As always, I became extremely irritable and cantankerous, not paying attention to my wife's feelings. I unknowingly created a lot of tension at home for months, until my wife cried out to someone I really respect.

Very quickly, she got my attention. We sat in her office for hours and had an open, frank conversation. It was an amazing eye-opening discussion under the inspiration and guidance of the Holy Spirit. We talked at length about standards and best practices, and came up with questions like:

- What do we consider good standards?
- Who sets them?
- Are these standards in line with God's word regarding marriages?
- Is there room for continuous improvement for husband and wife in this so-called standard?

- Coming from entirely different backgrounds, does this standard give consideration to the spouse who may be the weaker link?

- Is it just another selfish, self-centred, egotistical and vain characteristic of being preoccupied with oneself while undermining the feelings of the other person, which, if not handled properly, can cut short the lifespan of any marriage?

We made God the centre of our marriage from the onset and recognise that God is able to keep and perfect that which He started. So, we had to seek His help, particularly for me.

I love the NLV version of Phil 2:13. It says, "*...for God is working in you, giving you the desire and the power to do what pleases Him*". If you find that either of you lacks/or have certain attributes, or characteristics if you like, that may impact negatively on your relationship, you need God to give you the "desire and the power" to do what pleases Him.

We please God when we honour His word. One of such ways to please God is by loving and teaching your wife. Eph. 5:25 says, *Husbands love your wives, even as Christ also loved the Church and gave himself for it.*

My being excessively particular about almost everything around the house impacted our marriage so negatively, especially during the first year, I had to seek God's help and direction. God stepped in and started a maturing process in us, bringing us under His grace and giving me, in particular, a broader understanding that subdued my initial perception. I realised that, standards or no standards, we're all works in progress, and neither of us or anyone else in the world was near perfection. Human beings change over time.

One day I was driving and pondering over things I now recognise as very trivial issues when God dropped two questions in my spirit. "Why do you worry about "teachable" things?" He asked. "And why do you think the 'man is called 'the bridegroom'?"

Then He said, "You have your entire lifetime to groom your wife to be what you want."

An entire lifetime? I thought. But this simply means certain things in your lives will change over time, provided your spouse has a teachable heart and is willing to learn. Meanwhile, instead of paying attention to questions, I should be asking her like…

o *What do you want?*

o *How would you like this?*

o *What shall I do with this?*

o *Where would you like this kept?*

o *How do you like this meal served?*

I had paid more attention to her shortcomings, which was completely wrong.

With God's help, I realised that every single man and single woman possesses attributes that make us gravitate towards marriage. Then as the marriage progresses, we add on more attributes that should make the marriage work. For the woman, in particular, the arrival of children creates even more dramatic changes.

Honest advice from married couples

I worked on becoming patient and more understanding. By God's grace, I finally realised that since a married woman's life is centred mostly on her husband, children, and work; she is constantly under pressure. At that point, I came off my high horse and became more supportive, started listening more and showing more affection.

Four years into our marriage, not so old, not so experienced, I can undoubtedly say two things: God has been faithful, and it is not His plan for any marriage to fail.

God has a special interest in making our marriages work. As such, He commands husbands and wives to act in different capacities. Whenever our relationships enter the red alert zone, it is wise to ask God to lead the way. Just like the Psalmist wrote in Ps 61:2, *"From the ends of the earth will I cry unto thee, when my heart is overwhelmed, lead me to the rock that is higher than I"*.

Pray this way, and you will see God at work in your marriage.

The devil constantly launches attacks on marriages and relationships, but those that are founded on God's word and have God's backing will definitely overcome!

Married 13 years

When we met, we saw each other every day for a year. EVERY SINGLE DAY. And we would talk and talk and talk…

Seventeen years later, we've been married for the last thirteen, and we are still talking.

My honest advice? What has worked for us has been *words*.

Aside from touch, hugs and lovemaking, what keeps us together are words.

Talking. Talking about everyday stuff and deeper things like our faith or what fascinates us about our children.

I love my husband for the things he says to me; he compliments me every day. Just this morning he said something about my being one of a kind - I think he used the word "magical". Ha!

I might roll my eyes when he says those things, but I love it!

I think he also loves me for being a good listener. I listen to his crazy stories even if I have already heard them a hundred times!

Yes. Words. Definitely.

Talking, listening, and laughing. Compliments, 'thank you', 'I love you'. Encouraging words. Comforting words. Pet names. Inside jokes. Even arguments! Words help us create our own little world where there is just the two of us.

Our bitterest quarrels have involved harsh words, painful silences and malice; which are the opposite of the very thing that makes us tick…

Which brings me to my next piece of advice: Always go back to the things that brought you together in the first place. Remember why you fell in love. Remember when it was just the two of you.

Your being married doesn't mean you should deprive your partner of the wonderful side of you that attracted them in the first place. That attention you gave or care you took; that way of putting them first, or even the gorgeous red lipstick he loved so much… Always find your way back to that.

Finally, take them seriously, particularly in the small, quirky things -

Whether he likes to have his dinner at a certain time or wants you to come and keep him company while he is fixing some appliance,

if he doesn't like to eat alone,

or he likes you to stop whatever you are doing and welcome him when he gets home,

if she likes to talk on the phone,

or she likes you to go to bed at the same time,

- don't say to yourself, It's not that important" or "What's the big deal?" Being able to accommodate each other is always worth that minor inconvenience or slight irritation.

Honest advice from married couples

So!

1. Words.

2. Remember why you fell in love.

3. Accommodate each other's quirks.

STRENGTH IN COMPROMISE

Married 11 years

While house hunting before our wedding, (about eleven years ago), I really did not mind relocating as Milton Keynes was a fairly new and beautiful town. I worked out that from Monday to Friday, I would be at Medway studying for a Master's degree in Pharmacy. Then at the weekends, we could take turns spending time at our two homes until I finished my programme. This was me thinking any other arrangement on my part would be unfair as he had only just relocated to Milton Keynes from Bristol. Now he had finally settled into work and was enjoying his role, I needed to support and encourage him. He, on the other hand, thought that it would be too stressful for me to run two homes with such a busy academic workload. He'd noticed my involvement and dedication to my church family and the joy I derived from being there, and concluded the change would be too drastic for me. So, he moved to Kent and commuted to work.

My husband says that some advice my dad gave him has helped him through marriage; 'Remember that you were both raised by different parents in different settings, so your analogy, understanding and response to any issue would be very different. But if you both listen, are understanding, rational, and always ready to compromise; you should have no problems'.

This has proven to be so true… before concerns escalate into problems; we assess them carefully; recognising that our individual approaches would stem mainly from our culture and values, the way we were nurtured and raised, and that our unique natural responses or understanding of the present situation has defined our reactions. Compromise has therefore been the order of the day.

My husband and I have had to reinvent ourselves on many occasions. I am his biggest critic only because he always asks for my opinion on a website he has designed or is managing, a meal he has prepared, or a cake he has baked and decorated. My criticism was usually honest, constructive and to a very high standard. I would give my candid opinion unemotionally, not considering how he felt. After all, I was being truthful and desiring him to project the best of his skills. Meanwhile on my part, whether or not he was being sincere or helpful, I could not accept his feedback if he did not elaborate on what was good before mentioning areas I could improve on.

Over the years, I have learnt that constructive criticism is good, and honest, candid opinions are brilliant, but if they are not given in love, the experience leaves a sour taste in the other spouse's life. (1 Corinthians 13)

In conclusion, embrace and celebrate your differences. Remember, variety is the spice of life.

With Christ at the centre of your relationship, love has to be at the core of all your dealings. When loving your spouse becomes a challenge, (trust me, there will be such times), go back to the interpersonal skills you were nurtured with; the act of listening and consciously engaging in understanding your spouse.

Then the rationale behind any action becomes a bit more defined, and compromise will easily bring about a win/win situation.

ABOUT MARRIAGE4LIFE MINISTRY

The Marriage4Life Ministry was born out of deep appreciation to God for what He was doing in our marriage. We also felt the need to share with others how to enjoy marriage God's way.

Marriage4life provides couples with helpful tools to inspire, challenge and encourage them to build a not necessarily perfect, but great, amazing marriage.

Most people seem to have the idea that we can just "live life together" and everything in our marriage will be perfect. We thought this way too! We had no idea you had to work hard at marriage.

During our first few years of married life, we had so many more bad days than good that we thought it would soon be over. We tried to fix things on our own but didn't know where to start! There is no three-step formula to achieving harmony in marriage; but what I can say is, things began to improve after we BOTH committed to making it work.

Marriage4life is a movement committed to doing marriage God's way. We believe that with the right knowledge and insight, we can all experience the joy and satisfaction God intended us to enjoy in our marriages. And yes, we do it the Bible way because the author of the Bible is also the author of marriage.

Wherever you are in your marriage, do not give up! Keep working at it!

Join our Facebook live broadcasts on Sunday evenings for exciting live chats on pressing topics relating to marriage. These live events are very popular – with hundreds of shares and thousands of views.

You can also join our Facebook group (Marriage4Life Community), or like our Facebook page (@ marriage4lifeseries) to benefit from our teachings on marriage. You can also subscribe to our online marriage hub, The Money, Sex and Power (Prayer) Hub which provides in-depth teaching, exercises and

ABOUT MARRIAGE4LIFE MINISTRY

powerful prayer sessions thrice weekly on the things that can make or break even the strongest marriages. Visit our website for more details.

Marriage4Life Contacts:
www.marriage4life.co.uk
E-mail: marriage4lifeseries@gmail.com
Instagram: marriage4lifeseries

THE CONCLUSION OF THE MATTER

The reasons why we get married and the condition of marriages can vary greatly from couple to couple. The honest advice from couples in Chapter 16 of this book very clearly shows that! However, the reasons for staying married rest in one place: God. Marriage was His idea and that means it's a GOOD idea. If you're struggling or even if you're not, hold on to that and rejoice in it!

The words you use concerning your marriage are seeds, whether they are words spoken in prayer, during a conversation or shouted during an argument. Good words have the power to elevate your spouse and marriage. Bad words are also powerful, they can damage and pull down someone or something that was created to give glory to God. The words you speak should echo the words of the Creator of marriage. Just as you cannot reap a harvest without sowing seeds, if you fail to speak the right kind of words over your marriage, you can't expect to reap the right kind of harvest. Words are also the tools of effective communication, they reveal our thoughts (and misconceptions!) Sometimes we think the other person should *just know* how we're feeling or what we're thinking. Don't assume, talk! How else will they know how you feel about a joint bank account, why you took their words so personally or what works best during sex?

Perhaps some of the most pertinent actions to take as a married couple are the ones that fall under 'setting and keeping boundaries'. Boundaries protect the marriage from allowing the wrong people into it in the form of inappropriate relationships. They also protect us from getting caught up in the pitfalls that exist outside the limits of the marriage covenant: The Couples Danger Zone (Chapter 4).

The comparison between the Church as the bride of Christ and earthly marriages signifies the deep spiritual significance of marriage. This means that prayer, that connection with God that allows *His* will and *His* purpose to be carried out, cannot be over

The Conclusion of The Matter

emphasised. Just as Christ continually cleanses His bride, we also should continually pray for our spouses and marriages so that we can display the beauty of God's Kingdom as we stay married for life.

Finally, our prayer for you is that Almighty God will grant you the wisdom and grace needed to excel in your marriage and bring the best out of it.

Keep believing, your best days in your marriage are definitely ahead of you.